From the
CENTER
of the
EARTH

D0028907

Stories
out of the
Peace Corps

Edited by Geraldine Kennedy

Clover Park Press • Santa Monica • California • 1991

Clover Park Press

PO Box 5067
Santa Monica, CA 90409-5067

Second printing, 1992.

The following page constitutes an extension of this copyright page.

Contents

Maps

*To those who have
come from
and
gone to
the center of the earth,*

*Especially my mother
who has braved many crossings.*

Acknowledgements

The concept of publishing a collection of stories by former Peace Corps Volunteers was not ours alone. Other proposals had been circulating for years among large New York publishing houses. None of them would touch the idea. We thought its time had come. But during the three years in which we have been working on this project, pesky questions did nag us. Was there enough quality writing by former Peace Corps Volunteers? Could we get it? Was there a readership? Could we reach it? What did they know in New York?

This is not (quite) the story of the-little-engine-that-could. In real life it takes more than gumption to accomplish your heart's desire. As we slowly accumulated a substantial body of work many people advised and cheered. But there were a few whose enthusiasm, generosity, and timing kept the engine chugging. Patty Perrin, writer and friend, read every manuscript and provided countless thoughtful comments. Patty had served as "spouse of staff" in the Peace Corps in Afghanistan. John Coyne, novelist and former Peace Corps Volunteer, Ethiopia, provided access to many of the writers. Publication of his quarterly newsletter, *RPCV Writers*, has much enriched the link among far flung colleagues. My son, Peter, who with his siblings grew up on Peace Corps stories, shared his new computer and often saved the day with his insight into its counter-intuitive quirks. I am ever grateful to each of them.

Finally and foremost, this book would not have happened without my husband, Jim, who also read every manuscript, contributed his brilliant editor's ear and eye, and kept our household running during the tortuous production of maps and the heart-stopping decisions over cover design. He didn't do much else but keep the world upright and hold my hand.

frantically at the pink grains of aspirin caught in the honey sliding down her chin. "Please, please, take this, Wanjiro," I said.

It was just dawn and I couldn't see the mountain. It wouldn't clear that day. Dr. Spock said to give the baby a cool bath for the fever, so I woke Joseph to help me.

"It's malaria," he said when he saw her. "She must have a terrible headache, too, but it will pass." He put his arm around me and kissed the top of my head. "Our poor girl," he said. "She'll be all right."

He helped me with the bath and, as her temperature slowly dropped, she became less listless. At a hundred and one she took the syrup and baby aspirin. Joseph insisted on giving her a little chloroquin, even though I was afraid to, since we didn't know for sure if she did have malaria or the proper dosage for a baby.

"Let's take her to Nyeri, Joseph, to the doctor. I've never seen her like this." I put my head on his shoulder and he held me for a minute without speaking.

"Don't worry, my dear," he said, gently rubbing my back. "I know malaria. See, she is better already. Just keep her cool and let her rest and she will be fine when the fever breaks."

I had never seen anybody with malaria and she didn't seem to be shaking and chattering the way I had imagined malaria victims. But she was listless and hot and cried when I picked her up. "I still think we should take her in."

"She is a strong baby," he said, "and she'll be better in a few days. We don't run to the doctor for ordinary illnesses here." He left us sitting on the veranda and went to work.

When Jane came, she looked at Wanjiro and shook her head, clicking her tongue sadly against her teeth.

"Bwana says it is malaria, Jane. What do you think?"

She picked up Wanjiro and laid her cheek on the baby's cheek and then looked carefully at her eyes. "Yes, is malaria," she said.

"She is much better now," I said. "You should have seen her this morning."

Jane shook her head and laid Wanjiro back in my arms.

"Will be bad again tomorrow," she said without smiling.

When Joseph came home I begged him again to take us to the doctor. I told him what Jane had said, and he shook his head patiently. "Believe me, my dear, I know. This will only last a day or two more and then she will be perfect."

But she wasn't perfect. She lay listless in my arms the next day. I took her onto the veranda because it was cool out there and I came to believe that the fresh air and the protection of the mountain were essential to her recovery. I began to promise Ngai a number of things if he would just help Wanjiro.

I thought she was failing steadily but still Joseph wouldn't take us to the doctor. I was powerless before his calm reassurances and tried repeatedly to tell him of my fears. I begged him for my sake, if not for hers, to let us go into Nyeri. He refused. I began to hate him. I didn't understand why we couldn't make a simple trip to the doctor. "I want to take her home, to Minnesota," I said on the third day. "We can take her to the Mayo clinic."

He looked at me sharply. "You must learn to live in this country." He said there was trouble on the scheme with one of the machines and he left.

I stood alone and afraid on the front porch, holding Wanjiro and hating my husband.

Jane was waiting when I went back in the house. She had been in the kitchen, listening to us argue. "What can we do?" I said, crying as I looked at my baby, listless and pale.

"We will take her to Nyeri."

"But he took the car . . ." I began.

"Don't worry," she said. "Somebody will give us ride." She put her hands on her hips and stood beautiful as a sculpture, gazing at Wanjiro, her lovely lower lip protruding and the sad tongue clicks coming from her mouth. She was silhouetted against the rising mist. The mountain was still shrouded but the clouds seemed higher.

"I think we will see the mountain today." I said.

She nodded and smiled. "If we see the mountain, it is a sign Wanjiro will be well." She bent over and kissed Wanjiro swiftly on both cheeks. "We will go soon," she said. "I get ready."

I laid the baby in her crib. Her eyes fluttered continually and I couldn't tell if she were awake or asleep. I pulled on tennis shoes and a loose cotton dress that I had worn when I was pregnant. It would be a long, hot day.

When Jane returned, she said, "I will carry Wanjiro."

"She is too sick to be on your back," I said.

"Don't worry, Memsahib. I know how to carry her." Jane doubled a long strip of cloth and lay Wanjiro in it. Even though she was seven months old, she had lost weight and lay limp as a newborn. When Jane hefted her up, she didn't resist. Jane tied the cloth around her own back and neck and Wanjiro hung suspended in front, hammock-like. I put a baby bottle and a couple of mangoes in a bag and we were ready by seven-thirty. I thought of leaving Joseph a note, but our departure felt like an escape and I couldn't bring myself to tell him where we were going. I was afraid he would come after us and bring us back. He could easily catch up with us if we didn't get a ride by lunchtime when he came home.

It was a cool, humid morning. The sun was still low in the sky and the light filtering through the moisture in the air gave a dreamlike quality to the day. When I think of that day now it always has the look and feel of a dream: muted colors, slow moving bodies, faces of strangers emerging briefly in the mist to speak to us and then fading back into the fog. We had to walk eight kilometers to reach the tarmac. We would have no chance of a ride until then. I thought of all the times we had passed people walking along that road, people who had waved us down. Joseph always stopped and the first time I had said, "Do you think it is safe to pick up hitchhikers?"

He had laughed and said, "These are just poor people who need a ride. Nobody is dangerous here. It is my car, but everybody feels I must give him a ride if he needs it. They would do the same for me."

I remembered that and felt hopeful. We would get to Nyeri.

Jane was as heavy as I was, yet I could hardly keep up with her. I had to take quick little steps every twenty seconds or so and soon I was panting. But I didn't say a word because we had to get to Nyeri. Wanjiro hadn't moved or whimpered since we started. Jane kept one arm under her and she lay, slightly turned towards Jane's body, still and small. I tried to talk to her as we hurried along. "It's going to be okay, Baby," I'd say. "Jane and your mama are taking you to the doctor. We'll get you well." And then I couldn't talk for a while and would just concentrate on walking. The road was rutted and uneven and continually curved back on itself; our view switched from the plains ending in forest to the mountain rising into the clouds. Everytime we faced Kere-Nyaga, I evaluated the height of the clouds. We hadn't seen the peak since Wanjiro took sick. It seemed important that we see the mountain soon.

We were not alone on our trek. A woman with a small boy on her hip joined us almost immediately and walked with us for a few minutes and then started to talk to Jane in Swahili. Because of Jane's notoriety among the Kikuyu women, I was curious to know what they talked about. My Swahili was spotty, but as far as I could tell, the conversation was mundane—where are you going, who is the memsahib, what is wrong with the baby. The woman pulled back the cloth around Wanjiro and made that sad clicking noise with her tongue. I was to hear that sound all morning as people looked at my baby. They all did it, men, women, children, and shook their heads. You would think that it would get on my nerves, this incessant clicking, but it brought a lump to my throat for my sick baby. I had felt alone all my life until Wanjiro came and now, in my hour of desperation, these people walked with me, extended their hearts with indrawn breath and clicks of tongue. One woman kissed me before leaving us for a narrower path.

The road passed through a mountain stream. Jane took off her plastic shoes. "Is better, Memsahib," she said. As a fat girl growing up in Minneapolis, I never went barefoot, never played in the creek, because I was afraid of slipping or exposing myself in some unforeseen manner. I held my shoes and skirt in one hand and started cautiously across, my free arm waving to maintain my balance. An old grandmother caught my soft hand in her tiny hard one and led me across, saying, "Mzuri, Mzuri, Mzuri." She patted me on the back when I safely reached the other side. I was embarrassed and put my hand on Wanjiro's cheek.

"Jane, let's bathe Wanjiro, to cool her. She is too warm again." We sat under a huge chestnut tree and the children ran back and forth to the stream, soaking cloths. Wanjiro lay on my lap, and we stroked her thin arms and legs with the cool cloths and washed her face and head. Her eyes fluttered open and she looked right at me, I'm sure. She tried to smile but she was so weak and tired. Her lips trembled, trying to open. I looked towards the mountain. The clouds were rising.

By the time we reached the main road, most of our companions had dropped away and the few who remained turned in the opposite direction, on their way to the Friday market. Jane and I walked alone along the tarmac. I was carrying Wanjiro now, slung around my back and neck like Jane. I couldn't keep up with Jane's pace, but I needed to carry her myself. Jane knew that without my explaining and had nodded and smiled when I asked for the baby. I'm not strong and have this weight problem, and my heart was pumping hard the whole time, but the worst part was that Wanjiro was easy to carry. Like carrying a doll or a kitten. The cloth was hot on my neck and my arm under her got tired but she seemed shrunken and weightless, a butterfly baby that we carried along the Nyeri Road.

We walked for thirty minutes and no vehicle passed us. "Don't worry, Memsahib," Jane said. "The first one will stop."

The safari bus never slowed down. Jane and I bent towards the trees as one person, shielding ourselves and the baby from the dust. "I didn't even get my hand up," I said.

"Is all right," she said. "Those zebra cars don't stop. We waiting for a person by himself."

The mountain is never out of sight on the Nyeri Road. Even when we walked down in a hollow we could see it rising to our left. I thought of the lodge at Nanyuki where Joseph and I had met a party of climbers, men with axes and crampons who were leaving the next morning to go up. They were excited and said it was the best climbing in Africa, even better than Kilimanjaro, because of the challenge of Batian, the high peak. Joseph had been upset by the conversation and later told me that he thought the government should keep people like that out of the country.

I thought he was being silly. He knew as well as anybody that the tourist dollar is the number one source of foreign revenue, and at least they weren't shooting elephants. "Kere-Nyaga is more important than any elephant," he had said. I remember thinking that here was something else I would never understand. But walking that day under the protection of the mountain, I felt that it was sacred, a holy place, and if a man ascends the mystery peaks and takes pictures then the resting place of Ngai is violated. How can Ngai return to a place hacked by axes and despoiled by pitons hammered into rock? There must be some place for God alone.

We heard the Land Rover before we saw it, laboring up the hill, and Jane stationed herself across the road to flag it down. The car veered around her and stopped on the shoulder ahead. A white man in khaki shorts and shirt got out and walked back to us. "Your girl could get killed standing in the road like that," he shouted. He was Australian. "You got a problem?"

I was out of breath when I reached him and could barely speak. I pulled back the cloth to show him Wanjiro. "My baby is very sick," I said. "Could you give us a lift to Nyeri?"

He shook his head. "I'm going to Nairobi."

Jane had already opened the rear door of the Rover. "Okay," I said. "That's even better. We will go to the doctor in Nairobi."

"Lady, that's a hundred and fifty kilometers." He turned to walk back to his car.

I hurried after him, my heart pounding, Wanjiro swinging from me in her hammock. "Then drop us at Nyeri—it's only a little out of your way, and my baby is dying."

"Twenty kilometers out of my way," he said. "What are you doing out here with a native baby, anyhow?"

"Get in the car, Jane," I said. She was already in. I handed Wanjiro to her and crawled in the back myself. The man just watched us, not moving. I pulled the door closed, and he still stood there. Finally, he took off his cap, smoothed back his hair, walked to the driver's seat and got in.

"All right," he said. "I'll take you to Nyeri."

The ride was worse than the walking. The tarmac was

pitted and Wanjiro bounced around on my lap. It was as if the force of gravity couldn't keep her. Jane and I took turns holding her in our arms, away from our bodies so we could protect her from the jarring ride. She cried like a lost kitten, a soft, helpless wail, not as if she expected anybody to help her, but with cries forced out of her.

He dropped us in front of Dr. Bashal's office. "Allow me to pay you for your trouble," I said to him when we got out, fishing in my pockets for money. I did have money, after all, and he had made us feel like such beggars. But he waved me off and was gone before I had located a twenty-shilling note.

Dr. Bashal's office was filled with people. Jane, with Wanjiro, squeezed between two Indian women in saris on a narrow bench. A Kikuyu woman sat on a folding chair with two small boys in her lap, both with oozing sores on their legs. The man next to her slumped in a bent chair, asleep. Two men sat on the floor; three more stood against the wall. Everybody watched the door where the doctor would appear. Nobody spoke. The room was filled with the sighs and heavy breathing of the sick. Several people seemed as ill as Wanjiro, as if they, too, had waited until the last minute and then made a desperate effort to get to the doctor. I thought of Dr. Anderson's office at home— soft lighting, Muzak, and *The New Yorker*.

A young man in a blue shirt and blue work pants sat behind a white metal table in the middle of the room. He was writing in a large ledger.

"Do you have an appointment?" he said.

"No," I said. "My baby is terribly sick, we must see the doctor immediately."

He found a blank line with his finger. "Name?"

"Mary Wanjiro Nduta," I said. "It is malaria, we think."

He slowly printed her name in the ledger and wrote the number thirty-four next to it and wrote the number again on a square of white paper. He handed the paper to me. "This is your number. Can you come tomorrow at ten?"

I nearly burst into tears. "No," I said. "No. It is urgent. I must see the doctor today, now, right now." I banged my hand on his table and it wobbled dangerously. I clutched the table to steady it. "Look," I said, tears starting to form. "Look, see my child. Jane, bring Wanjiro here. Show him."

Jane came to the table and pulled back the cloth so the boy could see our baby. He looked at her and clicked his tongue against his teeth and shook his head. "Yes, I see. I will call you."

We waited a long time. There was nothing else to do. He called number twenty-two, and I thought I would die. A Kikuyu woman with a baby followed the boy through the low door. Her baby was smaller than Wanjiro and listless.

We were there an hour when Dr. Bashal himself came to the door to gaze about the waiting room. I hadn't seen him since he delivered Wanjiro. When he saw me on the bench, he spoke sharply to the boy at the white table, and the boy called number thirty-four next.

Dr. Bashal was one of those small, obsequious men with a pencil thin mustache and an ingratiating whine to his speech. "I am sorry you wait, Mrs. Nduta," he said. "If I had known you were here, I would see you immediately. Why didn't you tell my boy?"

"Please look at Wanjiro, Doctor," I said.

"Yes, of course," he said, and peeled back the cloth to look at her. He put his stethoscope on her thin chest, he gently felt her neck, examined her feet, looked carefully into her throat, took her temperature, weighed her, and then he shook his head.

"I am afraid that she is very sick, your baby," he said.

I could have felt sorry for him, he looked so apologetic, so helpless, but his words infuriated me. I knew she was sick. "What shall we do?"

"There is nothing to do. She has cerebral malaria." He washed his hands at the sink. "Perhaps if you had come sooner, but malaria, it is a bad thing and she has a rare case."

"Is there no medicine?" I said. "Can't you put her in the hospital?" I started to cry, to sob. I pleaded with him to give me hope, and he refused.

When I think of that day, it is all mist, except the twenty minutes in that little, white room. That is bright and clear and hard, a room with sharp edges and pure light from the bare bulb swinging overhead. There is no color, just white, and Jane's black face as she listened to him and his thin black hair and that black line of mustache under his nose. Even Wanjiro is white, deathly white, and the cloth that held her bleaches to lines and marks. He would do nothing.

We left. I remember leaning against the whitewashed building, sobbing and rocking Wanjiro, holding her to me, and when I looked up, I saw that the clouds were lower on the mountain. We stood on the street for several minutes. I couldn't face the trip home—begging for a ride, then walking the eight kilometers on the dirt road. I just couldn't do it. "We will stay here tonight, Jane," I said. "We will stay in a hotel." There was a little place down from the doctor's office. I knew Joseph would be upset for about a hundred reasons, not the least of which was that we went to this poor hotel. We should go to the famous Outspan to protect his position as an important man, but I couldn't face the mahogany paneling and the coffee on the veranda and the elegant buffet. I just wanted a room where nobody would notice me and my baby, and where Jane could stay with me. I didn't want to sleep alone with my baby in a beautiful room. So Jane and I got a room together and I asked her to go out and find somebody who would take word to Joseph on the coffee scheme, who would tell him where we were. While she was gone, Wanjiro and I lay on the bed and I tried to nurse her; but she couldn't hold my breast in her mouth, she couldn't suck, not even from the bottle. So I tried to give her milk on a spoon but it dribbled down her chin and neck. I thought of the spring when I was eight years old and tried to feed a baby robin that had fallen from its nest in my back yard, a terrified baby bird, unable to swallow. It died the next day in the shoe box padded with cotton and scraps of terry cloth that I had made for it.

Joseph came before dawn to take us home. I drove so he could hold Wanjiro. He held her in his arms, away from his body, anticipating the jolts, trying to smooth her ride. "Did Bashal say we could give her aspirin and chloroquin?" he said.

"Yes."

"Nothing else will help?"

"No."

"But, it's too late?"

"Yes," I said. "Bashal says it's too late."

Wanjiro died two days later, in my lap, on the veranda. It was the day the clouds rose above the mountain. We were sitting there watching her and watching the clouds lift off the high peaks, the white spot of snow brilliant in the tropical sun and the morning mist blowing away and the clear light shining on us all. I heard the sound of a weaver bird taking a seed, then a sigh from Wanjiro. Her eyelids fluttered once, then her mouth sagged and I saw her two little teeth.

I pressed her to my breast and wept.

"Ngai take our baby home," Jane said and pulled her apron over her face.

Joseph laid his hand on her head and looked at the mountain. "Praise ye, Ngai," he said.

Kathleen Coskran

Kathleen Coskran served as a teacher with the Peace Corps in Ethiopia from 1965-67, where she met her future husband Charles, also a Peace Corps Volunteer. They later spent two years in Kenya and now live in Minneapolis with their five children.

Born in Los Angeles, Coskran is a graduate of Agnes Scott College, Decatur, Georgia and has an MA from the University of Minnesota. She is currently an adjunct faculty member teaching fiction writing at both the University of Minnesota and Hamline University. Her story, "The Cook's Child," appears in the anthology, *The House on Via Gombito: Writing by North American Women Abroad* (1991 New Rivers Press). Her work has also been published in the *Clinton Street Quarterly*, the *Great River Review*, the *Utne Reader*, and *A View from the Loft*. Her book reviews have appeared in Minneapolis and St. Paul newspapers.

Since 1986 she has won the Loft Mentor Series, the Minnesota Voices Project Competition, the Depot Regional Writers Contest and the Loft Creative Nonfiction Award. In 1988, she received the Minnesota Book Award for *The High Price of Everything* (1988 New Rivers Press), a collection of short stories, in which "Facing Mt. Kenya" first appeared.

"I have often regretted that I don't have a deep sense of place or culture in my background. My family moved too much when I was a child. But I have learned that the vision of the outsider can provide a revealing slant on the world. As settings for my stories I have drawn on the two places I have lived which are most foreign to me, Georgia and Africa." The title of her recent first novel, *Ferenj*, set in Ethiopia, means foreigner or stranger in Amharic.

In 1989 an Artist's Fellowship from the Bush Foundation enabled Coskran to return to East Africa to research *Ferenj* which she has completed with additional support from the Minnesota State Arts Board. She is a 1991 recipient of a National Endowment for the Arts Fellowship.

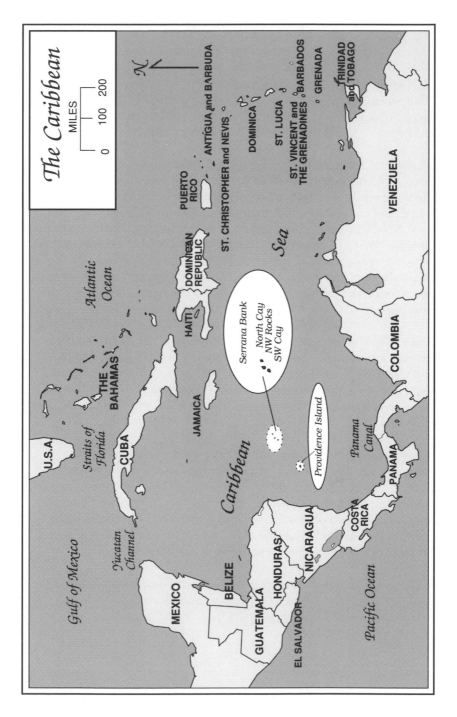

The Caribbean

MILES

0   100   200

U.S.A.

Gulf of Mexico

Straits of Florida

Yucatan Channel

Atlantic Ocean

THE BAHAMAS

CUBA

JAMAICA

HAITI

DOMINICAN REPUBLIC

PUERTO RICO

ST. CHRISTOPHER and NEVIS

ANTIGUA and BARBUDA

DOMINICA

ST. LUCIA

BARBADOS

ST. VINCENT and THE GRENADINES

GRENADA

TRINIDAD and TOBAGO

Sea

Caribbean

Serrana Bank
North Cay
NW Rocks
SW Cay

Providence Island

VENEZUELA

COLOMBIA

Panama Canal

PANAMA

COSTA RICA

NICARAGUA

HONDURAS

EL SALVADOR

GUATEMALA

BELIZE

MEXICO

Pacific Ocean

HUNGER

Bob Shacochis

Here in the cays away from Providence and the villages, there was a fellowship among the fishermen in their isolation. They did not mind that they were utterly alone and apart from the world—this was their life. The darkness completed itself around them, throwing the horizon across the water until it lay beneath them and they could walk it like a tightrope, toeing the distance underfoot. The great distance, the cusp of nowhere from which they worked a living.

Among them only Bowen, a white man and an outsider, did not share their history and so the solitude was more powerful for him. The sea had fuzzed out into invisibility, joined to the sky in a solid cliff of darkness. From where he stood on the cay that was like a shallow china bowl turned upside down on the water, the sea was still in his hair, in his eyes, everywhere, a wetness that wouldn't wipe away. There was nothing he could do about it. It pushed in when he opened his mouth to speak, and swept out again when he exhaled, stinging his tongue. It blew against him in the night breeze and added weight to his salt encrusted clothes. Air and water and small scab of land wrapped into each other and floated the men in the middle of darkness. Not even his grave held such magnitude for Bowen, not even that seemed so empty as this darkness. This was Bowen's feeling. It didn't worry him; it made him hungry.

On the mother ship *Orion*, anchored in the lagoon, a light in the galley flicked on. The light weakened and broke into particles only a short distance from the ship, a globe of blurry color suspended in the dense moisture. The silhouette of a man in a straw Panama passed across the yellow moon of the galley's porthole. The moon blinked. On the cay, matches were struck and placed to wood. A line of cooking fires wavered on the sand but the light revealed nothing more than the shapes of men crouched close to the auras of slow, lambent flames.

Bowen brought up more firewood from the beached catboat. He could see each arm of flame playing with hundreds of grape-sized hermit crabs that clicked and tumbled and rolled over onto their shells, escaping the heat and illumination.

The crabs provoked Gabriel. He grabbed any he could between his thumb and index finger and snapped them into the fire. He didn't want them crawling on his face at night, he said, he didn't want to awake to one of them picking its way across his cheeks or down his neck. In the flames, the tiny animals shrank in their red-white shells, burst and bubbled. It was a game Gabriel liked, but he was not a malicious man, not like Sterling, the murderer, who shot his mother's lover in the head with a speargun and raped the boys who were his cellmates in prison. Or Ezekiel, who was drunk all the time and let his wife and children go hungry. Everybody found it easier to forgive Sterling than to forgive Ezekiel. No one cared that Gabriel burned little crabs.

The night ran up the long shadows of the boatmen, merging with their black outlines as they tended the fires. Heavy iron caldrons and sooty Dutch ovens were shoved down into the coals as the flames waned. Into each pot was placed something different to cook. Men moved in and out of the shadows joyously, with clear purpose, racing back and forth to the boats from light to darkness to light again, carrying calabash shells brimming with portions of the first day's catch. The work they had done after setting up camp at the banks that afternoon was for themselves alone. No unseen white man could put a short price on the fish, not even on the tiniest mullet; no sprat had to be ferried aboard the *Orion* tonight and packed into the ice holds. The real work would come tomorrow when the Dutchman brought his scales ashore, and his tally book. But tonight was jubilation. Tonight every man was free to eat as much as he wanted. It was a spree, an eating fete, and everybody was happy. *We feedin weselves, mahn, Nobody else!* Bowen listened out of curiosity for a moment and then went about his business. *No dahmn bean big wife makin babies in she belly, five, six, sevahn kids cryin "poppa"; no grahnmuddah, uncle, ahntie or cousin John Robinson ten times removed and livin in de mountain so a boy must go up wit a fish fah de guy. No coolie mahn stockin de freezah in he shop, no tourist place on de mainland, no big goddahmn Texahn cowboy. We eatin everyting we got.*

Sterling's boys fixed the birds' eggs. They had pilfered them from the nests on Southwest Cay when the *Orion* stopped there earlier in the day to report to the four lonely soldiers sent to guard the fishing grounds from Jamaican poachers. With perverse authority the mainland government dropped off young recruits here for their first duty, left them with a sack of rice, fishing line and hooks, no boat and no shortwave radio, hundreds of miles from the shores of their homes, for six, eight, sometimes nine or ten months to enjoy the skeleton of a freighter, their only skyline, locked onto Pearl Henry's Reef.

It was this freighter, the *Betty B*, that the men on the *Orion* first sighted after their long passage from Providence. The massive wreck perched on the bleak, sun-scarred horizon like something ripped away from a city and dropped out of the sky to crumble and rust secretly, away from mankind. Captain Sangre anchored the *Orion* in water as transparent as coconut oil, over a sandy bottom dotted with thousands of conchs five fathoms below. One of the fishermen's catboats was unlashed from the deck and lowered over the side. The captain was rowed ashore to deliver the government permit, a preposterous formality, since the soldiers were helpless to enforce anything out here. Sterling and his boys went along to collect the eggs from the stick and pebble nests of the boobies, the frigate birds, the gulls and terns. The soldiers insisted that the eggs were under their protection and the fishermen couldn't touch them unless they paid a tax. After stone-faced negotiation, a bottle of rum, an old coverless *Playboy* magazine, and twenty pounds of cassava were handed over to the military.

From the rookery Sterling had gathered perhaps two hundred of the eggs speckled pink and blue and brown. After leveling the bed of embers, the boys boiled a ten-gallon can of seawater and threw in the eggs. The Bottom Town men stewed fish heads: triangular jaws gaping as the cartilage that held them melted, poking through the steaming surface of the liquid among an archipelago of eyeballs and flat discs of severed brain and bone. At another fire one man tossed the backs of spiny lobsters and their thick antennae into the vapor of his pot. The tails earned the best money and were saved for the Dutchman. All of the fishermen agreed the meat of the lobster, except for the fatty parts, was too rich-tasting anyway.

White gleaming wings of mashed-up conch simmered in another stew. Hot lard splattered and sizzled, foaming over dark orange sacks of roe. Turtle eggs that looked exactly like Ping-Pong balls boiled in the pot at the center of several men who poked a wire leader through the shells of uncooked ones and sucked out the raw yolk. Bowen was called over and given one as he passed cautiously by in the darkness on his way from scrubbing the fish slime from his hands in the wet sand at the water. He sucked the shell hollow but the egg felt syrupy and inedible in his mouth and tasted like something that shouldn't be swallowed. He spit it out in his hand to examine what was there, squatting down near the light of the fire. It was all bright viscid yolk threaded with a design of red capillaries. He slung the mess out into the night for the crabs.

"Dis stuff make yah seed grow straight, mahn."

Bowen returned to his own fire. Gabriel was watching intently as Mundo pitched a row of oval fish steaks into their pot: yellowtail and red snapper, hogfish, amberjack, gray vertical sections of barracuda. Bowen was surprised at the amount of fish being cooked, but he did not doubt the three of them would eat all of it. Mundo pulled plantains, brown and soft, and a giant yam from a burlap bag, cleaned and sliced these vegetables, added them to the stew with lime juice, salt, cornmeal dumplings, and a handful of garlic cloves, and small green cooking peppers. Bowen took a mouthful of stale water from a jerrican to wash the globs of egg gel from his teeth.

"It's beginning to smell too good, Mundo. I'm dying from the smell."

"Oh yes? If you staht to die, Mistah Bone, you must finish, too. Nobody to help you here, mahn. Who goin help? Tell me daht."

The overpowering aroma of the cooking, as distinct and potent and wonderful as the smell of water in the desert, rose from the pots and encircled Bowen, a warm, copious, life-giving atmosphere. As quickly as that, the sea that had racked him all day and all of last night, the presence that seemed to be a second skin he must learn to move in, abated. Freed from one sensation, he was enslaved to another. The sea was now part of his viscera, part of his strength, and Bowen knelt down to limit the pressure of hunger in his stomach, cloistering the force of it with crossed forearms. It was, he thought, the perfect gesture.

Mundo leaned behind himself into the darkness and re-emerged with a young hawksbill turtle, its eyes already shining with martyrdom, the flippers lashed together like hands in prayer with palm fronds weaved through cuts in the leathery skin. He held it by the tail over the pot and cut its pale extended neck with an easy pull of his machete. Black blood squirted into the stew. The act disgusted Bowen but he couldn't prevent the hunger from swelling up inside him, so foreign and portentous, unlike anything he had ever felt about food. It stunned Bowen to realize he had not learned that hunger was the pure voice of the body, of being alive. He did not know what had insulated him against this knowledge. He would rather have seen Mundo kill a worthless man like Ezekiel, the drunkard and child-beater, than butcher the magnificent sea creature that was so close to extinction, but he imagined the blood hot and salty as the brine that nourished it, the blood spilling from the opened neck of the turtle into his own mouth, seeping under his tongue, filling his mouth completely, gulping it down too fast to breathe until whatever was there that demanded so much was appeased.

Gabriel turned on the balls of his feet, calling out, "Who de hell burnin mahnchineel tree?" Mundo clamped a lid down on the cooking pot and the three of them moved away to investigate the source of the smoke from the poisonous manchineel wood. Bowen's face and arms had begun to itch and his eyes felt as if soap had gotten into them. The search brought the men to Sterling's fire. His younger boy, Jambo, was responsible for the wood and had mistakenly put a piece of the manchineel on the coals. He should have known better but nobody expected very much from Jambo. The can of eggs was pulled off and the water poured on the fire until the eggs drained. A fat column of smoke, spreading out around them, drove everyone upwind, rubbing their eyes, cursing and scratching.

"You a dahm monkey, Jahmbo."

"How daht boy chop dis wood ahnd cahrry it to de ship witout blisterin he hands?"

"How you get a boy like dis Sterlin?"

"Take ahn egg, mahn."

"Dey finish up cooking?"

"Dey feeling too hot."

"No, look. Dis one too juicy."

"Look here. Dis one nice."

"Dem eggs no good anyway. Dey too old, mahn."

"Dis one making a bird."

"Teach it to fly, boy."

The man studied his eggs for a moment and then flipped it onto the ground. Bowen bent over to look at it and saw the well-developed embryo of a man-of-war cooked white, almost plastic. Some men were tearing the shells off and popping the eggs down their throats without looking if the meat was bad or not. The close, wet air began to smell faintly rancid.

"Lord, dis guy nevah eat egg before. Sylvestah eatin de shell too."

"He mahd."

"How many eggs daht make, Sylvie boy?"

"Twenty-two." Crumbs and drips of brown-gold yolk stuck to his chin and fingers. "I ready fah someting new." But Ulysses said he had eaten twenty-three, so Sylvester ate one more out of pride.

Most of them had no desire to eat the eggs since there was an abundance of food at hand to reward patient stomachs after the long sail aboard the *Orion*. If the eggs were nice, they agreed, that was one thing, but they weren't: they were rotten. Watching Sylvester and Ulysses gobble the malodorous, runny eggs was good entertainment, but their own suppers were waiting. The groups wandered back to their own fires, stirred their pots and began to eat. Sterling was the only one who hadn't fished that afternoon. He thought everybody would appreciate the eggs and eat some and then share their food with him. Mundo called him over to take a piece of fish. His two boys, Ulysses and Jambo, went with the Bottom Town men because they wanted to smoke ganja while they ate.

Sterling, a tall, lean mulatto with stark eyes, sat down in the sand cross-legged, enamel dish in one hand, spoon in the other, stoically waiting to be served. With an empty oatmeal can, Mundo scooped into the pot and overfilled Sterling's dish until gray sauce oozed across the rim. Sterling's thanks were harshly whispered; the man seemed obligated to quiet gratitude. To Bowen, the relationship between Mundo and Sterling was a mystery. He had watched them closely ever since Gabriel told him it was Mundo's first fishing partner, Gabriel's predecessor, whom Sterling had killed. *Dis guy was real dahk ahnd Sterlin crazy from his momma sleepin wit such a blahck blahck mahn so he shoot him in de face ahnd den take a stone ahnd bahng him. Sterlin young ahnd foolish den, mahn.* At the time of the murder, Mundo himself turned deadly and swore he would avenge his mate, but for once the police reacted swiftly and got to Sterling before Mundo could. Now Mundo treated Sterling like an older brother would. Frequently they competed against each other in the water to see who was the best sailor, the best diver, the better shot underwater. But never on land. On land Sterling was most often deferential, even helpful. He knew that Mundo's white friend collected seashells and so the mulatto gathered them when he was working on the reefs, offering them shyly in his cupped hands to Bowen. Bowen was thankful Sterling would rarely look straight at him. There was an exclusive intensity in the fisherman's eyes, a dangerous fascination. When their eyes met for the first time, it made Bowen apprehensive, and now that he knew what Sterling had done, he could easily tell in his resinous, never-blinking eyes that Sterling had killed a man, that Sterling had watched a man die by his own power and will. It was like a brand.

With his spoon Sterling poked through the food on his dish, ostensibly waiting for it to cool, but he would not eat until Mundo had served himself. For everyone, the first taste was an immense relief, a reassurance that life was good and not only toil uninterrupted day after day. They ate from old cans or held tin bowls between their splayed knees, gouging the sand with their heels to make a trough for the bones and fat, rubbery skin. Mundo was the most serious eater. He had a big family—Gullie, his wife, and her seven children, his wife's parents and his own half-Chinese grandfather to support under his roof, plus a scattering of outside children, and though he fed them well, he always needed more to eat than he could get at home. He passionately sucked the grouper head he held catlike between both hands—it was bigger than his bowl—licking the delicate flesh of the cheeks and digging out the brain cavity with his fingers. The marble eyes were relished, the bones cleaned diligently: not a speck of meat eluded him. Gabriel would take a handful of snow-white steak and squeeze it into his mouth, chewing until it was all mashed up and half swallowed, and spit out as best he could the needlelike bones. He didn't bother that he lost large chunks of meat in the sand by doing this. Bowen was more methodical. Somewhat self-consciously, he picked the flesh free of bones before he took a bite. When invariably he missed one of them, he rearranged his mouthful with his tongue so that the bone was pushed to the forefront and then extracted, or failing this, he dropped whatever was in his mouth into the palm of his hand and pinched around until he found the damn thing. Judged by the pile of offal in front of him, knobs of vertebrae, long rows of dorsal spines like serrated knives, flaps of mottled skin, Bowen was eating the most, but the opposite was true.

Sterling talked a lot to himself while he ate, sometimes only moving his lips silently with the food, spit seldomly, and hacked without concern when a bone stuck in his throat until it blasted out. Sterling behaved like this occasionally, chattered away like an old woman, and then slipped back abruptly into his diffidence, embarrassed when he realized what he was doing. Like everyone else, he took second and third helpings and curled over his dish to slurp up the spicy gravy. Even Bowen, as careful as he was, had stains all over the front of his shirt, and his fingers and lips were sticky with the paste of boiled cartilage.

The men ate on and on. The darkness no longer seemed bleak but was comfortable and intimate, its vastness a barrier against any force that could possibly disturb the eaters. The fires dwindled to passive ruby clusters of coals, mystical and beguiling, as though something other than wood and flame created them. Stars began to drop through the black canopy of haze. The men did not so much decide to stop eating as they did fall thoughtlessly away from the pots exhausted, collapsing as athletes do after their greatest effort and concentration. They were stupefied by their extended stomachs and patted themselves delicately, croaking with gratification. For a moment Bowen experienced a release, an awakening of something sublime, but he told himself that was nonsense, he had misinterpreted insight or oneness for the dull contentment of a full belly. He let gravity take over and set him back into the broken coral that the sea had outcast to form the cairn of land where they camped. His dirty hands became gloved with flakes of cool sand. All around the cay the prone lengths of the fishermen groaned peacefully; with the increasing quiet, the hiss of the ocean surge on the reefs became audible, absolute energy leaching through the night from the interface of living earth and crashing, merciless water, ghost-white, somewhere in the distance.

One shadow still danced among the cooking pots, a faceless ebony shape that seemed intent on searching everywhere. It jumped from group to group like an obeah man, grunting and devilizing, its rasping steps circling closer to where Mundo and the other three sprawled around the remains of their dinner, not talking much, staring without expression or need for meaning into the sky. The spirit rose out of the darkness before them but nobody paid much attention. It was Ulysses, Sterling's oldest boy, a burly young man.

"Ahll right dere."

Sterling shifted, nodding to his son.

"Okay, Mundo."

"Ahll right."

"Mundo," Ulysses asked with quick, deep words that were almost unintelligible, "you got more to eat here?" The features of his round face were knotted together by a big ganja smile.

"Go look in de kettle," Mundo said with some annoyance. "Sterling, what's wrong wit dis boy? How's daht he doan get enough to eat?"

Sterling shrugged. Somebody was always asking him what was wrong with his boys. Ulysses eagerly removed the lid from the pot and peered in. From under his white cotton T-shirt, his black gut humped downward like the hull of a boat. He dredged the bottom of the pot but found only a few bones there and sucked them dry.

"I still hungry," he announced.

"Go beg a piece ah fish from Mistah Dawkin."

"Him finish up."

"Go ahsk Henry."

"Dey ahll finish."

Sterling said to his boy, "Go eat dem eggs. Lots ah dem left."

"Dem eggs bahd."

"What de hell, mahn," Mundo said sternly to put an end to it, "eggs still eggs, even if dey bahd."

This logic appealed to Ulysses's sense of gluttony. He retreated back into the darkness headed for the eggs, driven to clear the hunger out of his mind. From where they lay, the four of them half listened to Ulysses bumping into the gear, clanking over pots like a bear in his blind hunt for the eggs.

With his head back facing the stars, Gabriel sighed. "I like it like dis," he said. After a pause he continued. "But dis a lonely place. Dis place doan even smell like lahnd."

"I nevah been lonely. Not once," Mundo said, as though the matter was unimportant.

"Give me a cigahrette, Mistah Bone," said Sterling quietly. There was no need for politeness here away from everything, away from the world. Among the fishermen, all requests were straightforward and a man either helped another or he didn't. Anchored by satiation and fatigue, Bowen did not want to move. He invited Sterling to reach over and take the pack of Pielrojas from his pants pocket. Earlier he had been afraid that the men would not accept him in close quarters, but now he didn't care. Mundo and Gabriel were no problem because he worked with them, but back on Providence the others watched him cautiously, suspicious of his whiteness, never speaking to him. Mundo's own mother-in-law looked at Bowen as if he had come to steal the toes from her feet.

Sterling never took the cigarette from his mouth when he smoked. He rested back on his elbows and the ashes sprinkled down his bare chest. "Mistah Bone," he said tonelessly, "why a white mahn like you come to de cays?"

The question amused Mundo. He answered, "Mistah Bone come fah experiahnce. He want to study how hahd de blahck mahn work." He winked at Bowen and Gabriel as he said this and tugged his red baseball cap down clownishly over his eyes to indicate the absurdity and also the sufficiency of this reply. They did not pretend to understand why the world was the way it was, but among themselves they assumed that a man had good reasons, however offensive, for his actions. That was enough. Sterling's public showing of curiosity was easily dismissed, for Sterling was a strange man, a man who sometimes couldn't control himself. The fact was Bowen was there: He and Mundo had befriended each other. That was enough. The others were disconcerted by the enigma of a white man working with them; always and always black men had worked for clear-skinned people. That the pattern was disrupted was easy to see, but only Mundo accepted it nonchalantly as a natural course.

"I watch Mistah Bone takin notes," Gabriel spoofed, referring to Bowen's letter writing. "He come to write history of de cay in a big big book. He writin 'Dese bunch ah blahck men sail up to Serrena, go ashore ahnd eat like hogs!'"

Bowen laughed halfheartedly, satisfied that he didn't have

to say anything. He was convinced there was nothing to look back to—not here anyway, not in the middle of the ocean with men so different from him. Secretly, he trembled from a new sense of freedom, not prepared for the truth of it, faithless but full of modest expectation like a baptized sinner, carried to the river by force.

A shot of light, vanishing and then reappearing more brilliantly, drew their lazy attention to the camp of the Bottom Town men where a rag had been twisted into the neck of a soda bottle filled with kerosene and ignited, creating a phantasmagoria of gleaming skin, light sparkling from eyes and angles of metal, the choppy flash of a single thick flame, orange and greasy. The men could not relax for long. They had found their second wind, were standing and stretching and beginning to talk loudly.

"Sterlin, come play *pedro*, mahn. You got money to lose? Mundo, come play wit Sterlin."

Sterling yelled over, "I smokin dis cigahrette. You wait." The cigarette was only a nub of ash stuck to the roll of his lower lip. More kerosene torches flared from the camps of the other fishermen.

Ulysses came back clutching his stomach. He went to the white man first.

"Mistah bone," he pleaded, "you got some medicines?"

"What sort of medicine?"

"Stomach powdah."

"No. I don't have anything like that," Bowen answered. He was concerned though because Ulysses's stomach was squealing and making duck sounds.

"Where'd you find the duck?"

The boy began to wail. "Oh, Christ. Oh, me ahss, me ahss."

He turned to the other men for help but they wagged their heads without sympathy. Mundo said mockingly, "Dem eggs real good, eh?" And Gabriel turned to Bowen and asked, "You evah see a mahn eat like dis?" Bowen had no answer because he was fascinated by the clamoring coming from inside Ulysses.

Now Ulysses's indulgence was a big joke. He stumbled toward the slick black ocean, stomach quacking hysterically, and Mundo hailed the others to come witness the boy's trouble. The digestive storm at his center doubled Ulysses over and he crawled the final yard to the water, set his face into the glinting surface of the lagoon and drank like a horse, sucking the water into his mouth. The fishermen banded around him; their hooting chorus of laughter escaped out across the expanse of the sea, breaking against the austerity of the fishing grounds. Ulysses jerked his head out of the salt water and roared. The men catcalled above his noise.

"Look, look, him got enough food in he belly to feed ahll Cuba."

"Hey, Ulysses boy, you doan has to feed dem fish. Dey get plenty."

"Maybe he gonna be like dog ahnd eat daht mess right bahck up."

When Ulysses had finished purging himself, he rolled over and smiled up at the men, not like a fool, and not with shame, but like a man whose relief is genuine, a man reconciled past a moment of bad judgement. His father knelt down beside him and gently lifted his son.

"You bettah?" Sterling asked. "You ahlright now?"

"I eat too much of dose dahm eggs," Ulysses explained without much remorse. "Mundo say eggs still eggs even when dey snotty ahnd stink, but I eat too much. De first one taste good ahnd I must keep eatin dem."

Bowen stared at the boy and felt himself gagging reflexively. He felt his eyes squeeze tight with convulsion, his jaw thrusting away from his skull, his insides closing in upon him as though he, too, had stumbled to his hands and knees to gulp seawater the way a dog will chew grass to make itself heave. The sensation passed into a weightlessness, a rough freshness, and he turned away from the water and walked back to camp.

The men scattered to play *pedro*, to wash the cooking pots, to listen to Gabriel tell a story about a Providence boat that disappeared in Serrana with his father aboard. The wind fell off completely. A small flake of moon rose and gelled the sea. Out in the darkness the coral reefs relented and let the tide pass over them unbroken. Bowen lay on his blanket in the sand, waiting for sleep. The cards ticked loudly against the *pedro* players' soft conversation. The words spread entropically out into the night and somewhere, far out to the black sea, slipped underwater and were lost, flying like souls through an exquisite silence.

Bob Shacochis

Bob Shacochis served in the Peace Corps in St. Vincent and St. Kitts, Barbados, in 1975-76. He drew on his experience in the Carribean for, "Hunger," which first appeared in his short story collection, *Easy in the Islands* (Crown Publishers 1985).

Born in Pennsylvania and raised in Virginia, Shacochis received a BA in journalism, an MA in English from the University of Missouri, and an MFA from the Iowa Writer's Workshop. He has lived and traveled in Colombia, the West Indies, and Rome, Italy.

Shacochis is a contributing editor at *Harper's* and a columnist at *GQ*. His stories have appeared in *Vogue, Esquire, Playboy, The Paris Review, Outside Magazine,* and *Antaeus*. His second collection of short stories, *The Next New World*, was published in 1989 (Crown Publishers).

Shacochis is the recipient of the American Book Award for *Easy In the Islands*, the Rome Prize in Literature, the James Michener Award, and the Pushcart Prize. He is currently at work on *Swimming in the Volcano*, a novel set in the West Indies.

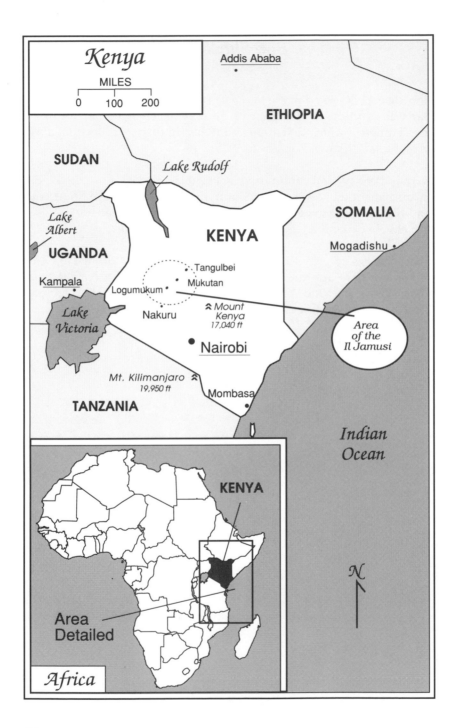

Kenya

MILES

0   100   200

Addis Ababa

ETHIOPIA

SUDAN

Lake Rudolf

Lake Albert

KENYA

SOMALIA

Mogadishu

UGANDA

Tangulbei

Kampala

Mukutan

Logumukum

Area of the Il Jamusi

Lake Victoria

Nakuru

Mount Kenya 17,040 ft

Nairobi

Mt. Kilimanjaro 19,950 ft

Mombasa

TANZANIA

Indian Ocean

KENYA

Area Detailed

N

Africa

MY FIRST LION HUNT

Tom Heidlebaugh

"**N**i *lazima*. It is necessary," my warrior friends assured me. "You must do it to become a man."

I sat under a thorn tree in the circle of young men, listening with the intensity of those who bank their lives on what they comprehend, as Ole Lenaya, with sparkling eyes, told us about the great lion hunts of his youth. The tree twisted heavy sunlight through filtering branches. I crouched against its rough bark, clutching the thin spear and broad, painted shield I had been loaned.

"We find the lion, we hunt him down." Ole Lenaya crouched low and scuttled around the rim of our circle, sweeping his lean arm as if clearing a place to stand.

"The *murran* circle the lion," he whispered. We all leaned forward to catch each movement, each word. My friends were all Il Jamusi *murran*, warriors in the same age set who had gone through circumcision and were on the way to manhood together.

"Then, *the one* can go in and kill that lion!"

Since Ole Lenaya wore a lion-skin cape, none of us doubted that he had been *the one* at least once.

"Sometimes the *murran* goad the lion with their spears so it will leap at *the one*. *The one* holds his shield before him, takes his *mkuki*, his blade, and puts it into the lion's heart." Ole Lenaya dropped to one knee.

53

"Sometimes, they go down together. Sometimes *the one* can grab the lion's tail and stab while he spins it around." Ole Lenaya jumped and spun in one motion. All the young men in the circle blew hard to show appreciation of his demonstration.

"Sometimes, if a man has a special reason," and now the elder looked deep into the eyes of each young man, "*the one* will wrap a blanket around his arm and when the lion comes will plunge his arm down the lion's throat. And with the other hand, put his sword into the lion's heart."

Suddenly the young *murran* leaped to their feet and began to wrap their robes around their forearms in imitation of the bravery of the old ones.

I noticed the scars like surf lines from a blood ocean on Ole Leyana's thin chest and up and down his left arm, which I could not doubt had been shoved down a lion's maw once upon a time, in the golden days. The bravery written on the old man's body was as great a lecture as the words he gave us in preparation for our hunt.

My friend, Ole Sambitche had been nominated *the one* for this lion hunt. He took on a serious posture and, with my borrowed sunglasses and cowboy hat, an exaggerated swagger. Spears and shields in hand, the *murran* and I took off. I was proud that, even without the years of preparation in ritual, hardship, and discipline, I was included.

The long-legged *murran* set a stiff loping pace. I fell in, imagining myself behind the ring of warriors surrounding the lion as Ole Sambitche stepped into the center to make the kill. Their years of running and fighting had given the lean *murran* an endurance my bulky hay-bucking muscles could never match.

"It's a long way to the lions," I thought as I began to fall back. Just before I collapsed in exhaustion, Ole Sambitche called for a rest. We stopped in the middle of a park-like area of thorn trees encircled by low bushes. I looked around at the group of ten youths, sweat streaming down their backs. They seemed to own the world. As each stood, balanced on one leg and a spear shaft dug into the earth, breathing easily, Ole Sambitche regaled them with a long speech in rapid Ki Jamusi. They laughed from time to time and glanced at me. Only Ole

Sambitche did not smile.

Then, in Swahili, Ole Sambitche approached me. "Mr. Onions, we have to continue the hunt. We will leave you here. Is that good?"

Too tired to feel any fear, I panted my agreement. Ole Sambitche seemed to have a second thought. His face was open and generous. "You wait here and we will go and find the lion. We will drive it to you and you can have the honor of being *the one*." I was stunned.

"I don't think I can kill the lion by myself," I tried to argue.

"Do not worry my friend," he smiled, "I will help you. You will be a warrior. I am a very good lion killer. You will not be in trouble."

Before I could answer, he turned and jogged off into the trees, his gang behind him. One by one, they waved and shouted, "good luck, Ole Lebarsosian. You rest. We will find the lion." They disappeared into the forest, singing their lion hunting song.

I was lost in Africa. Mr. Onions, Ole Lebarsosian, Arap Chemosit, He-who-jumps-up-and-down-and-laughs-alot. At the dances we put on at my house every Friday night, I had been given many names. The dances were designed to raise the spirits of the hard working Il Jamusi farmers who tilled the ten thousand acres of Red Creole Hybrid onions. They were raucous, until-dawn dances attended by hundreds of people eager to hear Magere play his magical guitar and me back him up with my clarinet.

In Milwaukee, we agricultural volunteers had all talked about our reasons for joining the Peace Corps. Most of the blacks in our group wanted to find some roots and bring them back. James Jackson had wanted "to take Mother Africa to the ghetto," where he hoped to be "a change agent, baby."

Some wanted to experience a third world country just lifting out of colonialism. Some wanted to see lots of animals. Many wanted to avoid the beginnings of absurd warfare in Viet Nam. Others wanted to do something useful, or get experience and build up their resumés for the future. All of us wanted adventure.

Me, I wanted a culture. I thirsted to be in a culture like an apple tree needed sunshine. A *National Geographic* photo of a lone Maasai loping across a vast plain drew me in and now here I was, waiting for a lion.

Back home, killing a lion was not required of me to be a man. But then, nothing really was, except making lots of money. Certainly the minimal training in holding a spear that Ole Lenaya had given me would not protect me. I no more wanted to kill a lion than I wanted to take on a Viet Cong.

From far in the bush I heard the first low growl. Hair I didn't even know I had stood up along my back. These Il Jamusi had found a lion and were really bringing it to me! Cattle lovers, farmers, jokers; tough and gentle, and reputed to be the most ferocious of warriors, my new friends were doing me the honor of bringing a lion for me to fight. I tested the branches of the thorn tree. It was called a thorn tree for good reason. I thought of death in a strange place.

Another growl and my adrenalin accelerated. I found myself oddly eager to actually see the lion. I practiced a thrust with my spear and tried falling under the huge shield I held in my left hand.

Another growl from behind me. Now there was no way to escape.

A lion cough from a bush to my right caused me to spin. Then a scream from my left and I leaped behind the tree. "Wait a minute," I thought, "how many lions?"

Ole Sambitche jumped joyously from behind his bush growling and waving my cowboy hat. From all around me the others leaped up, laughing and pointing at me. They had me surrounded and had been watching my fearful responses to each of their well-practised growls and roars. As they ran towards me I heard the ululation that was part of the famous Il Jamusi dances, full of pure energy and happiness.

"No lion, Ole Lebarsosian," Ole Sambitche grabbed me by both shoulders. "You will not have to die today. *Hapana kufa!*" He was very pleased with himself. He had been planning this ever since I asked to join them in a lion hunt. I laughed in relief.

We started back to the Il Jamusi village where I had parked

my *piki piki*, a 70cc Kawasaki motorcycle. My tall, elegant friends slapped me on the back, asking if I didn't wish I had my *piki piki* when all the lions came.

"I wish I had it now," I replied, thinking of the long way we had run and the long walk back. I had to endure more jokes about "no lions today—*hakuna simba leo*" which I parried with my feeble Swahili as I tried to keep up my part of this strange process of becoming a man.

Suddenly the round walls and thatched conical roofs of the village, with its thorn corrals, bomas and hide drying racks appeared. I realized we had been traveling in a huge circle all day and the jest had been pulled just a short distance from the village.

Ole Sambitche almost fell over when he saw my face. "You better give me back the spear now," he said. "The women will not know what to say to such a warrior." The group waved their spears and shouted as I handed back the weapon.

The cripple, Lebarton watched us stride into the circle of huts, roaring like lions. He limped up to us on his club foot. I knew he would never be taken on a lion hunt, even a snipe-lion hunt like mine.

He glared at our group as we approached.

"We didn't find a lion. We didn't kill a lion," I said.

"Of course not," he sneered. "That would be illegal. The government does not allow us to kill lions any more. Do you want us to get thrown in jail?" He used the Swahili phrase, *nyumba baridi*, cold house, and his eyes were as chill as his words. The warriors laughed.

Tom Heidlebaugh

As a Peace Corps Volunteer in Kenya in 1965, Tom Heidlebaugh served as field manager for the Perkerra Irrigation Scheme at Lake Baringo. He later edited texts for East African Publishing House and University College/ Nairobi.

While in Kenya, Heidlebaugh assisted Kalenjin writer, David Kiprono Ng'osos prepare a cultural history of the Tugan tribe, *Only The Sun Knows*, and several collections of folk tales, including *The Man Who Stopped Hunting*. He has also published a poem in an anthology of East African poetry, *Drum Beat*; and a novel, *Bus Ride* (East African Publishing House, 1967-68). In 1984 he prepared *Mountain Drawing*, a book on tribal storytelling for the Institute of American Indian Art, Santa Fe, New Mexico. "My First Lion Hunt" is from his novel, *A Bull Among the Tribes*.

"I returned from four years in Africa wanting to transport the sweetness of story to my own country," Heidlebaugh says. He has applied the discipline of story to education, and has used it as an administrative form in his work as program manager for the National Indian Youth Council and a therapeutic tool as a vocational rehabilitation counselor.

His essays and stories have appeared in *Akwesasne Notes*, *Nyota Afrika*, *La Confluencia*, and the *Clinton Street Quarterly*.

Born in Seattle, Heidlebaugh has lived and traveled extensively among the Indian nations of America as well as in Ghana, Kenya, France, England, Mexico, and Nicaragua. He performs, sings, and tells stories at conferences and American Indian gatherings.

Heidlebaugh lives with his Kenya-born wife Patricia, and their daughter, Meroë, in the state of Washington. He continues to work on an "unending flow of poems, stories, essays, novels, songs, pedagogical concepts, dreams and visions" while teaching in a prison.

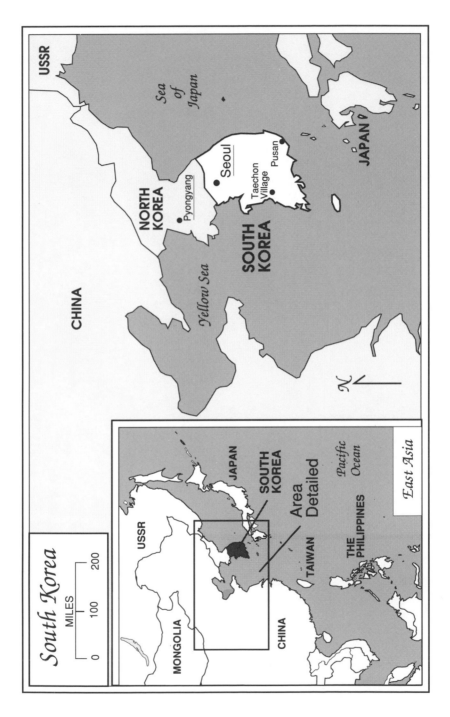

RETREAT

Richard Wiley

The American has been here for months now and I was worrying about the fact that I had still not spoken to him, worrying whether he had noticed and whether he thought my silence an unkindness of some kind, when he walked up and spoke directly to me. I was astonished. He spoke in Korean, and though his words were strange, I understood them. He was asking me if I would like to join an evening English class that he had organized for the benefit of the teachers of the school.

I was so taken aback that my mouth hung open like a stupid old bird's. I said, "I have enough trouble with Korean," an expression that made the American smile, and one in which I have taken some pride now that I've had time to think it over. "I have enough trouble with Korean." Considering that I did not expect him to come to my desk and that I had no time to prepare what I would say, I think such a statement exhibits my good training pretty well. It is disarming, it is self-effacing, and it is polite. All in all, it is a very good thing to say, and I have learned from it the lesson that spontaneity is not always bad.

The truth of the matter is that I have been wanting to speak to the American, but I have been muddling around, imagining myself walking up to him and delivering some comment like, "Good day, sir," which any fool knows will almost always bring the response of "Good day." I might have said something about the business of the school, of course, but I was afraid anything like that would be too complicated and he would not understand. How wonderful, then, that it is all cleared up now. "I have enough trouble with Korean!" Not bad at all.

I have noticed that my fascination with this American is not so far removed from the fascination one feels during a courtship, and that makes me pause and chuckle. How is it that I have become so enamored with the man? It is as if the Chinese circus has come to town and I am spending all my money to stand inside its strangest tent.

Written on the slow train to Hong Song, as I work my way up the valley to see my younger brother.

At the back of the school there was a big room housing the library, and Mr. Soh, once a week, was the school librarian. There weren't many books in the library, but it had the school's best stove, and for that reason Mr. Soh had reserved it for Bobby's special English class, the one he had been promising to teach ever since his arrival in town.

By now Bobby understood, of course, that teaching in Taechon Boys' Middle School was a worthless occupation for a Peace Corps volunteer—even his best students would end their formal education after ninth grade. He had been assigned there, he had come to realize, simply because the Ministry of Education had been given the job of placing the Peace Corps volunteers and had not known what to do. He was a commodity, a badge of improvement for the community, and nothing more.

But if he was going to make the best of it, he asked himself, why not teach a special class for teachers and adults, since there were some who were interested? Headmaster Kim, when he heard about it, wanted to charge the teachers and pay Bobby extra for his work but Bobby said no. His only other stipulation was that they not go drinking after class. He was healthy again, and he wanted to stay that way.

The first students to enroll in the special class were Mr. Soh, Mr. Kwak, and Mr. Nam. Bobby asked the headmaster and vice-headmaster if they too would like to join the class but they both declined. "English is the language of the young," said Headmaster Kim. "I have enough trouble with Korean," said his assistant.

On the first night of class, Mr. Soh went back to school early to relight the library fire, and the rest of them followed later on. When Bobby left his room, walking up the pathway leading to the main road, he envisioned himself not so much as a teacher but as a leader of discussions, keeping everything simple but letting the others do most of the talking. He wanted this to be something he did well. His students would learn that the English language, too, was flexible and could be used creatively by someone with control. Never mind that the students were of vastly different abilities; he would trim his lesson to include them all.

Bobby was walking quickly, looking at the moon and thinking over the potential difficulties of the class, when the Goma appeared from the shadows, underdressed as usual and ignoring the cold night. Though Bobby had been living with Policeman Kwak for several months, he had continued meeting the Goma occasionally, so seeing him pop up wasn't surprising. There was no place for him among the teachers, however, and Bobby told him so.

"Teach me too," said the Goma. "Big-time class start right now."

The more Korean Bobby learned, the more atrocious the Goma's became. "No Goma," he said. "This class is for the teachers, not for you."

"Please," the Goma said quietly. "It is my only chance."

Bobby stared at him. His only chance for what? He couldn't speak Korean well, he had never been to school, and the teachers would surely be insulted by his presence in the room. Still, he had spoken very well just then, and Bobby knew all too clearly what being an outcast was like. Did the Goma really think he had some kind of chance? He didn't even have a winter coat, let alone any kind of chance.

"Please," the Goma said, seeing something like real consideration in Bobby's eyes. "If I learn English I can go to America, be your boy. Or I can hang out with army, get lost, find my way."

Bobby looked at him. "The teachers won't like it," he said, and at the same time he realized that he was going to take the boy along.

"Screw the teachers," said the Goma, reverting to pidgin again and making Bobby wince. What was he getting himself into?

When they entered the library, the others had already arrived. The stove was hot and a pot of barley tea was steaming on top of it. Bobby tried to make light of the Goma's presence, but even Mr. Kwak seemed surprised by it. "He's only here to listen," Bobby said in English. "Think of it as our good deed." And the Goma, as if concurring, scurried into the corner, making himself small.

Bobby sat in a chair that the teachers had placed at the head of the table, closest to the stove. Mr. Lee and Miss Lee were beside him, and Mr. Soh was at the far end with Mr. Kwak and Mr. Nam.

"All right," Bobby said. "Let's try this. Let's speak only English, or let's try to anyway. Let's not use Korean except for clarification."

Bobby said this twice, first in English, then in Korean, and everyone nodded, faces expectant and bright.

Bobby had a notebook with him, but all he'd managed to prepare was a list of possible discussion topics: The upcoming U.S. election, popular music around the world, Korean-American relations, the recent defection to the South of a North Korean big shot. He was about to suggest that they start with something simple when Mr. Nam stood up and began walking around the table, passing out books. "Here we go," he said.

Bobby wanted to object, but Mr. Nam astonished him by handing a book to the Goma, who was still slumped against a bookcase at the rear. All right, Bobby thought, if Nam can be democratic, I can too. He looked down at the title to see what Mr. Nam wanted them to learn. *American English Hollywood Style*, said the print on the cover of the book.

"Mr. Nam . . . ," Bobby said.

"I know, I know," said Nam. "But give it a chance."

When he spoke he looked at the Goma again and Bobby knew he was trapped. He opened the book at random, and as he turned the pages he discovered that the book was essentially a collection of old American slang phrases, each one followed by a Korean explanation and by stick-figure drawings depicting the social situations in which the phrases could be used.

"Okey doke," said Nam, "Here's one, page twenty-six. What do such phrases mean?"

Everyone turned to page twenty-six, and Nam, before sitting down again, patiently found the correct page for the Goma. There were three English phrases on page twenty-six, in the middle of a sea of tightly typed Korean. All the expressions were wrong and Bobby looked up, hoping someone would come to his aid. No such luck. "Explain please," said Mr. Nam, "each expression in turn."

Mr. Kwak had a faintly bemused smile on his face, but the others looked at Bobby as Nam did. "Nothing unreasonable going on here," their expressions seemed to say.

Bobby read the first phrase out loud, and to his surprise they all repeated it in unison: "Please may I have intercourse with you?"

He had them repeat the phrase one at a time, skipping the Goma, and reasonable renditions of "Please may I have intercourse with you?" rang around the table like a song. These folks had had language classes before.

"All right," he said, "what does this expression mean?" There was a moment of hesitation, but then, to his surprise, Miss Lee raised her hand.

"Yes?" Bobby said. "Miss Lee?"

"It is polite method of asking for conversation," she said in good English.

Bobby's eyes lit up. "Yes!" he said. "That's right!"

"What, then is the difference between 'intercourse' and

'speak?' " asked Mr. Soh.

"Ah," Bobby responded, "there's a big difference. Once they were similar but now they are not. Now we say speak every time."

"Except when being formal," said Mr. Nam.

"No, Mr. Nam. 'Please may I speak with you' is now accepted in informal and formal situations as well, you can be sure."

"What about when addressing the president of the United States?" Mr. Kwak wanted to know. His enigmatic smile was still there, but Bobby couldn't read his intentions.

"When addressing the president of the United States one should never say, 'Please may I have intercourse with you,' " Bobby answered. Then he added, "Of this I am sure."

All five of them were taking notes, and even Mr. Nam seemed willing to alter the wording of his phrase now that Bobby had told him he should. Bobby could see, out of the corner of his eye, that the Goma was working his mouth a little too, turning it in completely unaccustomed ways.

Miss Lee got up to bring everyone tea and they went on to expression number two: "I always was born with a silver spoon in my mouth." Bobby read the phrase to them and they repeated it heartily. Maybe this isn't going to be so bad, he thought.

"This one comes a little closer to real usage," he said. "Except for that word 'always' in there. It means that the speaker was born rich, that he has always had money."

"Ah ha," said Mr. Nam. "You said 'always.' "

"Yes," Bobby answered, "but to say 'always was born' gives the impression of repeated action and we are only born once. It is an occurrence that ends once it has happened."

"Ah," said Mr. Nam, "but we can be reborn," and Mr. Kwak nodded, conceding, for Bobby, that point.

What was Bobby to do? If Nam was trying to draw him into religion, he would not be drawn. He looked at Mr. Lee, the only one as yet not to speak, but Mr. Lee shook his head. "Too deep," his expression seemed to say, his face froglike in the warming room.

Bobby took another breath and said slowly, "Perhaps we can be reborn and perhaps we cannot, but the expression in question has nothing to do with that. It has to do with whether or not the speaker was born rich, and one can only be born rich once. Thus, no 'always.' "

The English he had used was pretty complicated, but no one seemed lost. Mr. and Miss Lee both nodded as if accepting the logic of the point, and Bobby stared at Mr. Nam, a bluff, hoping he'd shut up once he saw the challenge in his eyes. No such luck.

"Ah," Nam said quietly, "but when one is reborn one is reborn with abundance, and abundance means 'rich' so 'always was born with a silver spoon in my mouth' means to be reborn, resplendent in the riches of God."

Bobby looked down at the Korean surrounding the expression in the book. Surely nothing like what Nam had said was represented there. What should he do? He had wanted this class to be his first real teaching success. The final expression leapt off the page as if mocking him, but he plunged ahead heedlessly out of his depth.

"Beat me daddy eight to the bar," he said, but this time there was only scattered repetition, for Mr. Nam and Mr. Soh were silent at the other end of the table.

"What the hell does this mean?" Bobby asked, and Mr. Kwak laughed. "It was apparently used when asking someone to dance," he said. And then he added, "I only know this, however, because I read a little ahead."

"Jesus Christ," said Bobby, but though he'd spoken under his breath, that was too much for Mr. Nam.

"Jesus Christ?" Nam said. "What do you mean by that?"

"Nothing, Mr. Nam," said Bobby. "I don't mean a goddamn thing by it." Nam leapt to his feet pointing down. "Jesus Christ! Goddamn!"

"Oh, shit," Bobby said.

Mr. Nam pulled at his collar with the hand that wasn't pointing and began to gag. He jumped up and down, his finger slicing the air like a concert master's.

Bobby tried to apologize for the language he had used but Mr. Nam would not quit. He stood there sputtering Bobby's obscenities back at him and then, plugging his ears against Bobby's attempts at reconciliation, he ran around collecting the copies of his book and bolted from the room. A moment later Mr. Soh ran out after him.

The rest of them sat there staring at each other. Bobby had wanted the evening to go so well. The expression on his face was one of desolation, and in a moment the three remaining teachers began touching him, bringing their chairs closer and telling him not to worry.

"Never mind," said Mr. Lee. "Nam is always like that," and Miss Lee nodded too, assuring Bobby that indeed he was. Then Mr. Kwak spoke.

"Now that that is over, what the three of us would really like is simply to discuss things with you." His tone was soft but there was an urgency in his voice that made Bobby think that everything, thus far, had gone according to his plan. "You know, we are Koreans," Mr. Kwak continued, "and there is much that we would like to say and cannot because we are afraid. Mr. Lee and Miss Lee, for example, would like to tell you about themselves. They both understand the English we have used and can make themselves understood when necessary." Mr. Kwak paused to see if Bobby was listening, if he had gotten over the shock of Mr. Nam's leaving, and then he added, "Do not misunderstand. We need not speak in English. As a matter of fact, we are all proud of your magnificent ability in Korean. But if we call it an English class, don't you see, that will make things easier all around. As for the real language of our discussions, it should be the truth, whatever the tongue."

Mr. Kwak stopped speaking and waited, but Bobby was stunned. Mr. Lee and Miss Lee both seemed to have transformed themselves from hopeful English students, from wide-eyed physical-education teachers, into conspirators, and Bobby didn't know what in the world to say. Peace Corps volunteers weren't supposed to be political, but then these people weren't asking him to be political, were they? They were only saying that they wanted to dispense with form and talk openly.

Miss Lee had brought cake with her and she placed a fat piece in front of each of them, giving the Goma one from the portion she had brought for Mr. Soh and Mr. Nam. She looked at Bobby and said in a quiet, offhanded way, "You know, Mr. Lee and I are lovers."

It was only the second time Bobby had heard Miss Lee speak in English and he was sure she was mistaken in her choice of words. Perhaps "lovers" like "intercourse," had gone around the bend and come back with its meaning trimmed. Lovers meant friends perhaps, or maybe it meant that they were engaged.

He sat up and said, "What do you mean, exactly, when you use the word 'lovers.' Maybe you mean close friends?"

Miss Lee was still for a moment, but then she gave him a quizzical look. "Forgive me," she said. "Lovers. Mr. Lee and I are lovers." She emphasized her words carefully, and then Mr. Lee, hoping to make everything clear, closed his right fist and ran his left index finger in and out of it quickly, in an incredibly obscene way. Bobby could feel himself growing red. "OK," he said. "I get it. Wow."

"We were lovers when we lived in Seoul," Miss Lee continued, "and we are lovers now. We will be lovers always, I think."

"So why don't you get married?" Bobby asked.

"Because our families are against us," Miss Lee said slowly. "Because Mr. Lee and I were sent to Taechon as punishment. We were banished for our activities when we were teaching elsewhere."

"You were banished together?" Bobby asked. "That was awfully nice of them."

"No, no," said Mr. Lee. "Banish apart. Come together two years later, secret-like."

"Mr. Lee changed his name," said Mr. Kwak. "After two years in another village he changed his name and was able to secure his position in Taechon. "I was the intermediary. Miss Lee had been here waiting for him all along."

Bobby looked at Mr. Lee. "What was your name before you changed it?" he asked.

"Mr. Lee," said Mr. Lee, and Bobby's double take made everyone laugh.

"Mr. Lee changed his given name, not his surname," said Miss Lee. "No need to change Mr. Lee. It is so common."

Though only minutes before Bobby had felt terrible about the disruption of his class, now he was feeling fine. Mr. Kwak seemed to sense the return of his good mood, for when he spoke again he said, "Please, Bobby, do not get the wrong idea. None of us are criminals here. Mr. and Miss Lee were student leaders, and I am only a country man struggling with my languages and my verse. We are not North Korean sympathizers at all. Like most Koreans we are in favor of reunification someday, but all we want now is a clear voice. My thoughts concern the tragedy of our land, and Mr. and Miss Lee demonstrated to demand open elections, nothing more. One man, one vote. Do you recognize that slogan?" He sat up a little and grew intent. "Even now," he said, "even this conversation we could not have in Korean in any of the houses of this town. Any hint of curiosity about our brothers to the North, any comment concerning real elections with real candidates, would be dealt with harshly, to say the least."

Mr. Kwak had raised his voice and he sat back down now, a little chagrined at being carried away. "As you can see," he said, "this is something about which we care rather deeply."

Bobby certainly believed that, but when he looked at the Lees, with their bright eyes and their good health, the consummate physical-education teachers, he had a hard time reconciling himself to the fact that they were dissidents and lovers. Only Mr. Lee's gesture seemed in favor of it.

"So what is this English class for?" Bobby asked. "What do you want me to do?"

"What can you do?" asked Mr. Kwak. "What do you think?"

"Nothing," Bobby said. "The Peace Corps is just what it seems to be, nothing much, nothing special."

"Are you sure of that?" asked Miss Lee. "Some of us have wondered."

Bobby leaned back and smiled, looking at the Goma to

share the wonder of it with him. What could they possibly think the Peace Corps was? If they had any idea that it was the C.I.A., as some Koreans believed, then they'd never have told him anything like they had. Surely they didn't believe it was some kind of leftist organization. What else was there?

"No, no," said Mr. Kwak, reading Bobby's smile. "We only want to get it off our backs. We know that you are what you appear to be. We only want a friend, an outlet. Otherwise everything stays bottled up."

"Get it off your chests," Bobby said, "not your backs." It was the first English mistake he'd heard Mr. Kwak make.

"Ah, yes," said Mr. Kwak, "quite."

Bobby didn't know what to do. They had been told in Seoul that they were to stay out of politics, that such involvement, in fact, was a sure ticket home. But was this politics? A couple of lovers who wanted free elections and an aging intellectual who wanted an outlet for his thoughts? No, this was not politics but ordinary human contact of the kind Bobby had rarely experienced at home.

"OK," he said, "so what should we talk about?" For some reason the three of them laughed.

"About poetry," said Mr. Kwak.

"About football," said Mr. Lee, "and judo."

"About Mr. Nam's funny book," said Miss Lee, "and about the Christian movement in general."

Bobby looked back at Mr. Lee. "I'd like to study judo," he said. "I've been thinking of talking to Policeman Kim."

"Talk to me," said Mr. Lee. "I can teach."

As suddenly as that the spirit of the little meeting had grown warm and humorous again, all three of them clearly glad to have said what they had, to have finally gotten what they had to say out in the open, off their backs or chests or whatever.

Bobby was about to suggest that they tell him about their hometowns when Mr. Kwak looked at his watch and said that it was time to go.

"What? Already?" Bobby asked.

"Yes," said Mr. Kwak, "time flies."

When they began looking around for their coats the Goma

grew a little frantic. He closed his dirty fist around Miss Lee's sleeve and looked at her downright lewdly. "Beat me Daddy eight to the bar," he said. Mr. Nam had forgotten to take the book from the Goma, and Bobby was amazed at the sound. The Goma's intonation was accurate, his pronunciation clear, and in his eyes could be seen the tiniest flicker of real intelligence, before he dropped Miss Lee's arm and danced in little circles, moving around the room like a clown, picking up the last piece of cake and shoving it into his pocket like a fool.

Richard Wiley

Richard Wiley was born in Fresno, California, and received his BA from the University of Puget Sound. He has also completed an MA at Sophia University in Tokyo, Japan, and an MFA at the University of Iowa.

As a Peace Corps Volunteer in Korea in 1967-69, Wiley taught English as a second language. He has lived and traveled for extended periods in Korea, Japan, Nigeria and Kenya.

Wiley's novels include:
> *Soldier in Hiding*
>> (Atlantic Monthly Press 1986)
>
> *Fool's Gold*
>> (Knopf 1988)
>
> *Festival for Three Thousand Maidens*, from which his story,
>> "Retreat," is excerpted. (Dutton 1991)

He has received the PEN/ Faulkner Award, Best American Novel of 1986 for *Soldier in Hiding*.

A member of the Associated Writing Programs and PEN American Center, Wiley's work has appeared in *Story Quarterly*, and the *New York Times Book Review*.

Wiley is a professor of English at the University of Nevada, Las Vegas, where he is currently at work on a novel set in Nigeria.

NEIGHBORS

Maria Thomas

Another white woman lived in the house before I did and everyone stared at her, too. "You get used to it," she told me. When I first moved in, kids shouted *mzungu* at me in case I didn't know I was different. They chased me to the bus stop begging for candy, a kind of extortion, but I held out and they gave up. The woman who lived here before had warned, "Watch out what you get started. Some things you can never get yourself out of." She was talking about the water, not candy. She was talking about my bathtub, one of the few in the tiny tract of houses that had indoor plumbing. Everyone else had to get water from the tap at the corner, which, unfortunately, was dry a lot of the time. And so, from my predecessor, I inherited the responsibility of keeping this tub full at all times, a neighborhood reservoir.

One day, desperate for a bath, I forgot the tap was dry and plunged in, sank into the cool water there with the same sigh I might have used back in Vermont on a December night, where the water would have been hot but no less welcoming. There was that same reassuring lap, water licking porcelain like lake kissing shore. It gave me a lost feeling, dense with nostalgia. Out of my window where the sun did what no northern sun could do, banana leaves were layered in succulent greens and the pervasive smell of grated coconut charmed the air. I lathered up and sang.

It was the sight of my feet that suddenly accused me of polluting the neighborhood water supply. By the time I reached them with the soap, small eddies of mud and other things were loosening. Just the ring around my tub was enough to make me certain that even in the garden this stuff would be considered toxic waste. At that guilty moment, however, I got a brilliant idea of installing some kind of water tank out by tap number 7, a community self-help project. Though I am a linguist, a lexicographer brought out to build quick vocabularies in places where language and technology were out of kilter, everyone assumed I was a Peace Corps volunteer. My neighbors often brought me things to fix or came looking for medicine. They expected me to supply them with seeds at planting time. One of them thought that I had come to teach them all how to screen their windows. But I never did anything like that and wondered if they suspected my presence had some nefarious purpose beyond the learning of their language. If it hadn't been for the water in my tub, I probably wouldn't have known anyone.

Sophia Mturi, who lived directly behind me, listened carefully to my idea. "We can all work together and build"—here, speaking Swahili, I had to use an elaborate construction—"a very large bucket in which to put water laid by for the future."

"Ooo," she said, "*tenki.*"

"Yes, *tenki,*" I replied. Like a badgered member of the Académie Française, these rank Englishisms haunted me. Tenki. Benki. Motaa caah.

Sophia, a sanophile with no spigot, had six kids and a husband, Palangyo, to wash clothes for. She washed everything, in fact, and was known to visit my cistern many times on dry days. Palangyo worked as a cook in a European house and whenever they had cocktail parties, Palangyo emptied all the glasses. Though he insisted his employers were Spanish, Sophia believed they were French because they didn't get around to eating supper until past ten o'clock, and once it got that late, Palangyo didn't bother to come home. Americans, she said, were the best people to work for because they ate at six o'clock, paid the most, and had machines to wash and dry the clothes, machines that their servants could always sneak in to use. Sadly, Americans always fired Palangyo because the memsaabs couldn't stand his drinking. Sophia figured that her father had benefited most from her marriage—twelve cows, since she was literate and also, by her own admission, beautiful, big and plump with the fine creamy skin attributed to people who ate plaintain three times a day.

She liked the idea of this water tank, but was wary. "Who will keep tricky people from taking too much and leaving nothing?" she said, though she was the most likely to offend.

I said I thought that in the spirit of self-help and cooperation, if everyone worked together, no one would steal since stealing only meant stealing from yourself.

She looked. "I can see you don't know Africans," she said.

We made a list anyway, of what to do and how to proceed, and the sight of the writing, some of it her own, fired her imagination. We needed a plan, she said. *Mpango.* From *kupanga*, putting everything in order. She wrote: one, two, three. We needed to find out how much it would cost. We needed to get official permission. Finally, we had to get the money. It even fired my imagination, for I had been thinking more in terms of a few steel drums and a length of hose. When there was water at the tap, you filled the drums; when there wasn't you used what was in them. Sort of like my tub. Suddenly I did feel like a Peace Corps volunteer.

The other neighbors, ones who used tap number 7, were interested enough to agree to attend a meeting. Helen and Norbert Manda, who lived on my left, were generally keen on improvements. They had put little wooden shutters on their windows, for example, and kept potted plants in tins on their front porch. It was usually on weekends that Helen came shyly and politely to my door with her small kettle. Then in order to compensate for the inconvenience, she had me to tea. They both worked in "offices" it was said and had enough money to acquire lots of things, most of them second-hand and broken on purchase. They lived in constant search of spare parts and repair men.

Paul Ntila, who lived on my right and called me "Sistah" or

"Missus," depending on the view of Americans held forth in the daily news, kept his water stored in plastic jugs and when those ran out, went to stay with friends. But he was committed. "Because of the others suffering," he said , "I will join."

Sophia told me that instead of a wife, Ntila had a radio-cassette, reasoning that since the cost of this machine certainly equaled the price of a bride, he had chosen the one over the other. We sat at my table with sheets of lined paper making lists and checking names. Sophia could only write by leaning over with her head at the edge of the table looking up toward her hand because, she said, she had learned it that way, a tiny girl at a very big desk. Mr. Ntila, she said, worked at the Ministry of Works, which made him rich, though he bought nothing but cassettes to play in his machine and late into the night. The music kept Sophia awake, wondering where Palangyo was, night after night. To that end, she had scrimped and saved and finally got her husband a used bicycle so he could speed back and forth and come home regularly.

Sophia had drafted the neighbors who lived on either side of her. The papers that she carried around and worked on and the adherence of the Mponji household, consisting of elders, gave weight to the project, an air of legitimacy. Baba Mponji had two wives, one old and one young, and he rented the living room of his house to Baba Abdullah, a mullah, and his old and only wife, Mariam. On the other side was Candida Rweyemamu, who had her husband's extended family living over there and who needed as much water as she could get. They had built ramshackle additions to the house to fit everyone in. Two of her husband's nephews lived in a cardboard box covered with plastic out behind the kitchen.

Everyone attended our first meeting at tap number 7. Though it was a stinking hot night, there was a Northern Hemisphere energy, a fit of cooperation, chaired by Sophia, who frequently jotted on her pad or pretended to, since I knew her upright angle made it impossible. She selected Ntila and me to determine the costs, which she called "billings" in English, though God knows where she got the word. Perhaps from an Indian. Helen and Norbert Manda, who were to get the official permission, served us all tea. Then, in the middle of a long speech about hope and the future that Baba Mponji was delivering, Palangyo appeared and our meeting collapsed. He announced that he had been badly beaten and robbed of his bicycle. He'd been coming home late the night before when thieves jumped out of the bushes. He had to spend most of the day at the police station.

Sophia ran to him. A voice rose, Baba Abdullah's, complaining of the times and the fall of man. Kids, excited by the upset, raced, pulling on each other's clothes. Words were lost to me then; I could only sense them falling like rain around me. Helen Manda had stayed back and was looking at me and I could tell she was so embarrassed. She had a long, gentle face. Her hair was plaited in a simple style, her dress remarkably fresh and clean, a nun's aura, sad and neat, with clasped hands.

On our pricing trip, Paul Ntila talked about Palangyo's bicycle, abandoned in a village near the bay, found and then returned to him by the police—two improbable events. The bicycle had been damaged, yes, but *found*. And *returned*.

"In fact," I said, "this morning when he got on it, the chain fell off." A crisis, in which Baba Mponji, known as a mechanic, and three of the Candida in-laws worked for an hour to get the thing back together and running. Ntila, who was wearing a cravat and sunglasses, said something about simple people and simple machines, but his English wasn't good enough to make the thought clear.

We took a sketch of the water tank to a welder down in the market. Chickens picked among the stacks of charcoal braziers and recycled tin cans made into kerosene lamps. I loved these places where people made the things they sold, where it seemed you could order anything. Elementary in all the good connotations of that word; you knew where what you got came from. I would miss this when I went home, where manufacture meant something else. Ntila was talking to the welder who leaned, as if exhausted, against a pile of bedsprings. We also consulted a carpenter since the tank was to be raised on legs so that the women could easily draw the water into their buckets from a tap at the bottom. In the end, we figured we needed a total of five hundred shillings, which, divided by each household, would be about eighty-five shillings or by adult person, as Ntila suggested, about thirty-five shillings: the cost, he said, of two cassettes. He frowned. "I will have to pay a bride price soon," he confided.

That night near the tap we presented our results. Helen and Norbert Manda thought it fairer to pay by adult person, but everyone else looked glum because even twenty shillings seemed too much.

"As for myself," Candida said, "I use all my money. If I save some aside I will only use it."

"This is why we are poor," Sophia complained.

Candida's sister-in-law suggested time payments, "We will slowly-slowly give our money to Baba Abdullah. Of all the men, he is most honest." The baba held his hands in a grateful manner and touched his heart.

"When the time comes," Sophia told me after the group had separated, "and you count this slowly-slowly saving, you will only have to know how to count to zero."

I thought about it for a minute and said, "What if I charged money for the water in my tub? Until each person paid? It could be a way to save," which on the surface sounded like a great idea.

"But the ones who are short of money, how will they pay, and how will you tell them no?" She used the term *shati-mahney*. Now, I love languages the way some people love vintage wine or gourmet food, but I could never turn in anything like *"shati-mahney"* to my fellow professionals with their computerized word hunts: they were purists and *shati-mahney* was plonk. What you guzzled when you wanted to get drunk.

When Sophia saw some of the others a few days later at the kiosk, they reached a consensus that paying for the water in my tub was a good method of raising funds and decided informally that I could simply hand over what I collected to Baba Abdullah for safekeeping. I was to hand out credit and debit chits to keep the record. *Cheti,* as they were called after the colonial fixation.

Norbert and Helen Manda were good for it right away and

paid the whole balance on the first tea kettle. Even Ntila appeared, flush, saying he had sold some of his cassettes and a pair of old shoes to raise the money. He winked because I knew why. He had a sense of duty, wanted to be a good neighbor, he said, and took a saucepan of water to boil his rice.

He asked me, "Are you a Peace Corps?" What he said was Peace Corpse.

"No," I told him, "I work at the Swahili Institute; they're looking for new words to keep up with the modern world."

"You?" He looked puzzled. I wondered if it was the idea of me or the idea of the project. "But you don't speak very well. A little, but not _very_."

"In fact," I said, "you don't need to speak at all." This would have been hard to explain. It amused him though. He shrugged and left. We had stepped out of my door in the last of the afternoon. Flies were hanging in the shade of banana leaves, too hot and tired to buzz, and the dust had puffed, fine as powder, to form a cloud around us. The whole atmosphere made me happy.

Very early next morning, I was awakened by loud voices out back. Palangyo, who had fallen from his bicycle, was wailing that he had broken a leg. He told the story that he had mounted the bicycle to go to work when the seat fell off and the tires went flat, which dropped him to the ground. By the time I got out there, Sophia and the kids were all around poking at the fallen thing as if it could be prodded back to life. One of the Candida nephews appeared with a wrench, and Baba Mponji was fetched out of bed to fix it again. Palangyo's uniform, of course, was filthy, and the whole affair threw Sophia's compulsive wash schedule off. She came looking for water in my tub, chattering about how she thought the whole business with the bicycle was odd. Suspicious. There were plenty of words in her language for this. "How can a seat fall off, a chain fall off, tires go flat?" she asked.

I thought, somehow, she already had the answer in mind. "Bad things happen in threes," I told her lightly. "This is what we say in English. A proverb. The chain, the seat, the tire. This will be the end now.

It wasn't the end. The following day when Palangyo started out to work, he noticed the handlebars felt warm to his touch. They grew hotter and hotter as he went along and then, before he had gone very far at all, the bicycle started to shake violently and threw him off. Sophia's three eldest children and two of Candida's ran out and brought it back. By this time, Sophia was convinced that someone had put witchcraft on the bicycle, and although it was not a very modern thing to do, against her religion and the law, she went straight to a witch doctor.

Candida, dipping water on account, told me that, according to the witch doctor, the bicycle had been stolen that first night not by humans but by fiends, agents of a powerful witch who was living in our midst. "Someone paid this witch," she explained, "someone who is jealous of Palangyo and wants him to lose his job."

"What will you do about this?" I asked her.

"First, Sophia has to find out the witch," she said.

To do this, Sophia had been given a pot of a certain dark, oily, foul-smelling substance which she was instructed to paint on every door in the neighborhood, a small dot of it. Whenever a person who knew the identity of the witch passed through one of the doors, he or she would immediately fall down and be temporarily paralyzed. At this point he or she could be grabbed and made to reveal the identity of the witch. Candida had seen with her own eyes (she pointed) this very method work in the case of a thief who had stolen her towels. He fell down and could not move until he revealed where the towels had been hidden.

Sophia got busy painting dots. She even painted one on my door, which I went in and out of several times to prove my innocence. She sneaked a dot onto Ntila's door while he was away visiting his mother in Bagamoyo. Helen and Norbert Manda, however, refused to allow her to touch their door. I heard them arguing in loud, dry voices, using Swahili I didn't understand but that I got the gist of. Not only was witchcraft against the law, Norbert shouted, but Sophia was a stupid, ignorant fool to believe such things. I heard him tell her to go back to the bush, that it wasn't witchcraft, it was simply Palangyo having the d.t.'s. From my window, I saw Sophia run from them, her cream complexion deepened with a fury like hand-dipped chocolate from the vat.

Sophia was convinced by this that Norbert and Helen had something to do with the curse on Palangyo's bicycle. Their refusal to have the medicine painted on their door was an announcement of guilt. She went from house to house like a vigilante. She even suggested that Helen herself was the witch. Why didn't Helen have any children? How did Helen have so much money, so many things? Candida said that one night she had seen a creature fly to the roof of Helen's house carrying something heavy and dark like the body of a child. One of her nieces corroborated the story, saying that the creature had a red comb like a rooster and smelled very bad. And so it went in the hot afternoons, sometimes around my tub, while Palangyo stayed home and skipped work. Who knew what story they were telling his employers, Spanish or French?

It was Paul Ntila who had the singular bad luck to trip and fall in his doorway on the afternoon he returned from his mother's while several of the Candida minions were standing by to see. Though he was not paralyzed on the spot, the event reverberated through the neighborhood and the man was grabbed. I listened from my window. Sophia ordered him to name the witch. Ntila didn't know any witch, he said. He didn't know anything about the queered bicycle. During all this, someone from another block rushed into his house, snatched his radio-cassette and threatened to smash it if he didn't talk. Was it like this in Salem, I wondered?

Baba Abdullah arrived, dressed in his mullah's outfit, and cried, "Stop this, please! Please! Please!" His arms were raised.

Norbert Manda, who passed on his way home from work, shouted, "I will call the police! You will all go to jail!"

"He's protecting his wife! Let the girl tell us what she saw, what flew over this man's house." But the girl was running away and Norbert stormed off, swinging his briefcase like an angry executive.

I heard a voice then, perhaps Abdullah's repeating, "Please, you must not throw stones!"

"If you throw stones," I called out to them, "then I'm going to get the police." I ran outside.

"Get them!" Ntila shouted. "That one over there has stolen my radio-cassette."

Baba Abdullah had reached my side; he touched my wrist. "I am embarrassed and ashamed," he whispered. "You must think of us as ignorant and foolish children." He warned the crowd, "God forbids this!"

One of the Candida nephews, a small one who lived in the box, asked me, "Have you witches in America?"

"You are a nincompoop," the baba told him, in English.

There was a lull. No one seemed to know what to do next. Except Ntila, who made a quick break and ran. In an instant he was gone. All the little gardens in our neighborhood had been planted to corn which was tall enough now for a man to slip and dart through, into the old banana plantation, down to the river and away, the route of thieves. The crowd scattered as if to give chase, but in fact, except for Sophia, who had a real stake in the palaver, no one else was interested enough to bother getting scratched up down there.

Helen's long face hung in the evening shade, a darker patch in the shadow of her porch. "You must wonder at us." She spoke as I came closer. "We are such terrible and stupid people." She spoke English beautifully.

"Actually, it's the bicycle I wonder about," I said.

"Yes, it is strange. Perhaps Palangyo has made it all up. You don't understand our people. He could easily make it all up," she said.

"But why?

"Because of jealousy."

"Jealousy?" A word I had been hearing. *Wivu.* Stronger in Swahili for its two syllables.

"Yes," she sighed. "So his enemies would be blamed."

Draped by a blanket of children, Abdullah was still guarding Ntila's door when the police arrived, followed by Ntila in a taxi.

"This is terrible foolishness," Abdullah said, "forgive us." He opened his palms.

Ntila was angry, scowling, looking around. The police took names, but it was really the radio-cassette Ntila wanted—his tapes and a few other valuables. In the end, he stood in front of the baba and said, "I want my money, the money from the water tank, thirty-five shillings." He looked accusingly at me, as if I had a part in all this.

"And mine as well!" Norbert Manda said from behind. "*Yangu pia!*"—so that he could explode that *p* like an invective.

"No, no . . ." Helen was saying. She was all eyes ringed black and a hairdo of sprung twists. Her hands were clasped like prayer.

But the baba had opened his pouch and was emptying the water-tank account. A few shillings remained, clinking sadly.

"We have fallen low," he said. In his robe he gleamed like a white column. A black prayer mark on his forehead glowered at the crowd.

We were left suddenly with the quiet night. I squished a trail of ants noiselessly following the path between our houses. Ntila's was all locked up now, unlighted, a gloomy thing.

"He'll move away," Sophia said. "Now we can never find out the witch."

A breeze. A smell of blooming, maybe jasmine, a reminder of sweet times. I thought of my tub in there, full of cool water. The taps were running and the bath was mine. I could soak the night away, just a little melancholy with the thought of that drained purse.

"But you don't really believe in witches, do you?" I asked Sophia.

"What do you know?" she said. She walked away, past the bicycle, chained there to the tree and worthless, like stock in a bankrupt company. She tugged listlessly at the bewitched handlebars.

The witch doctor said the only thing they could do now was to destroy the bicycle itself. Baba Mponji and crew did this according to a detailed set of instructions, wrenching and pounding, as Palangyo looked miserably from his window.

Sophia's job, once the fiendish machine was dismantled, was to deposit the various bits of rubber and metal here and there in very secret locations. She also had anointed sticks, which she was supposed to bury six steps from each of the four corners of her house. But even so, the curse could not be foiled and Palangyo did lose his job, though some of us thought it was because he had been absent so much.

"Any course will come so if you make it," Norbert Manda said.

And Helen said, "Mr. Ntila has moved away. He came in a pickup and collected all his things." She seemed sadder than usual, which purified her even more.

A couple with a baby arrived to rent Ntila's old house, and because they need gallons of water to wash diapers, the idea of selling the contents of my tub to raise money for the storage was revived. We gathered once again on a cloudy evening near tap number 7, which had been dry for three days. Even my tub was empty. Baba Abdullah made a long speech about everyone sharing troubles. I could only understand a little and the proverb that I knew: "The rain does not fall on one roof alone." I was introduced to the group as a Peace Corps volunteer. There was a good feeling again. We sat on wooden chairs and drank a pot of millet beer that Mama Mponji had brewed.

Palangyo's bicycle was still with us. Kids in the neighborhood were claiming that at night they had seen it, a phantom, going along with no one on it.

"I saw a *shetani* riding it," one of the Candida nephews said. A chameleon *shetani* (Did I know the one?) familiar to everyone by its popping eyes and long, furious tongue.

"You cannot see *shetani*," Candida said. If you look on a *shetani*, you will drop dead instantly."

"Then what did I see?"

There were a few drops of rain then, though no one bothered to move. It felt too good.

"Rain," I said, perhaps stupidly.

"Yes," Baba Abdullah agreed.

"Good," Sophia said.

And then, as more came, people started to move along, to get their basins out to catch what they could. In the morning, as I went to look for new words in my computer, I'd see them all out, washing cloths in the puddles that gathered in the hard, baked earth.

Maria Thomas

Maria Thomas (Roberta Worrick) was born in New Jersey in 1941 and lived in Ohio and Massachusettes as a child. She was a 1963 graduate of Mount Holyoke College, studied painting in Florence, Italy, taught at New Mexico State University and received an MA from The Pennsylvania State University.

By 1971 she was teaching in a private boarding school in Vermont. It was from there that she and her husband, Thomas Worrick, an agricultural economist, then the parents of a five-year old, went to Ethiopia as Peace Corps Volunteers. Joining the Peace Corps was, she later said, one of the "Series of Last Resorts and Desperate Alternatives" at a time when her husband was unable to find any other work.

The "desperate alternative" became the bend in their lives. Following their Peace Corps service, they continued to live and work in Nigeria, Tanzania, Kenya, Liberia, and other African countries. Thomas' writing began in earnest in Africa. In 1986 and 1987 she returned to the United States as a Wallace Stegner Fellow at Stanford University. Immediately following her time at Stanford, Thomas published a collection of short stories, *Come to Africa and Save Your Marriage* (Soho Press, Inc. 1987), in which "Neighbors" appeared, and her first novel, *Antonia Saw the Oryx First* (Soho Press, Inc. 1988). Both won critical praise.

Thomas regularly published stories and articles, including a report on Ethiopia for *Harper's* for which she received a citation from the Overseas Press Club. She also won a number of short story prizes including the *Chicago Review* Annual Fiction Award, the National Magazine Award, and the *Story Quarterly* Fiction Prize.

Fluent in four languages and much in demand as a translator, Thomas accompanied Worrick, Congressmember Mickey Leland and eight others on a 1989 plane flight in rural Ethiopia. None of them survived a hillside crash.

The Maria Thomas Prize for Fiction has been established in her honor by the National Council of Returned Peace Corps Volunteers. Thomas' novella and last stories will be published posthumously by Soho Press in September 1991. The book is entitled *African Visas.*

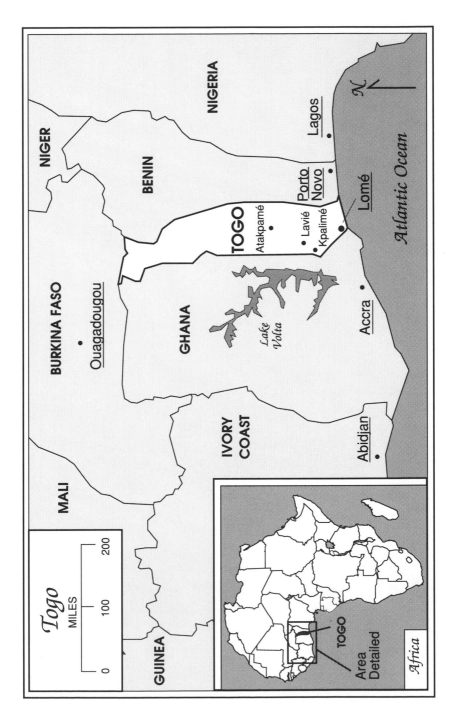

90

KHAKI AND GOATSKIN

George Packer

I had come to teach. Five days after arriving in Lavié, armed with a few rough lesson plans sketched in a thin copy book and a map of the U.S. from the American Cultural Center in Lomé, I drove my Peace Corps-issue moped off the *yovomo* onto a rutted trail, past the chants of the primary school, and into the grounds of the Collège d'Enseignement Général.

It was 6:45 am. The entire school was assembled on the field, the students in rows facing a flagpole, the dozen teachers in a knot to one side, under the mango tree outside the principal's office. Seeing me, a few teachers waved.

It was not yet hot but clear it was going to be. The grounds of the school were a rough terrain of dirt, cut grass, and fringes of shoulder-high grass that had grown up over the summer and not been cut back. The woods encroached on the far end of the grounds and seemed about to catch three adjacent classrooms of one building in its tangled branches and creepers. The buildings were ranged haphazardly over the terrain: three long cinder-block structures with window and door openings but no windows or doors, and corrugated iron roofs breaking out with rust. A pair of open-air thatch shelters stood alone in a field. The entrance to the principal's office next to one of the cinder-block buildings was paved with concrete and lined with flowers; behind the office stood a rutted dirt basketball court with a pair of netless hoops tilting precariously.

"Attention for the mounting of the colors!" a boy yelled as the sound of my moped died. Another boy began yanking a rope to raise the green, red, and yellow Togolese flag. I got off to lock my bike next to a Suzuki, and a Kawasaki with a sticker on its gas tank: "Fifteen years of Peace," it read, the words forming a halo over the image of President Eyadema in military dress.

Three hundred and fifty voices, so quiet I didn't hear them begin, were singing the national anthem. "La Togolaise" has a sweet melody, a little like the French children's song "Alouette," oddly free of the bombast of most anthems. The voices rose and fell:

> Si nous sommes divisés,
> Nos ennemis nous vaincront . . .

They stood, splashed by the pink light of morning, in a dozen neat rows of twenty or thirty, a sea of khaki. Every boy wore khaki trousers and a long- or short-sleeved khaki shirt; with their flared collars and epaulettes, they looked like a troop of underage black recruits for some European desert battalion. Every girl wore a khaki skirt—which fell below the knees, sometimes to the ankles—and a white blouse. The girls' uniforms gave an inch of room for variety, and those girls from families with a bit more money than the village norm could display it with lace frills around the bodice and on puffed sleeves, a pair of gold earrings from Ghana, imitation-leather shoes from the Bata store in Kpalimé instead of the usual flip-flops. But hair plaiting was forbidden. The general impression that the rows and rows of students gave was egalitarian, uniform, dull. Most girls wore simple blouses or even white T-shirts.

Few collections of Americans this age—about eleven to twenty—could stand scrutiny in the sun, lightly dressed, and come off looking as good as these. Somehow the swarms of village kids with rounded bellies and skinny limbs—the ones who survived childhood—turned into boys with rock-hard stomachs and shapely girls. But the striking thing about them was the variety of sizes. Girls with full bosoms and hips towered over flat-chested prepubescents, boys under five feet stood in line with young men who looked like stevedores. It was hard to guess which line was the youngest class, the *6ième*, and which the oldest, the *3ième*.

Peasants sent their children to begin school as late as the early teens, after years of fieldwork. Once here, they were routinely flunked, even twice or three times a grade. The *doublants* and *triplants* had the bored, slightly mocking looks of the disgraced; they stuck out among their diminutive class-mates as if their larger size were the mark of shame. In the older classes, success was visible in the small bodies of a few kids who had started early and whipped through without flunking (at least one-quarter were in the family of Monsieur Amouzou, the government coffee and cacao agent). Technically speaking, there was no such thing as a *quadruplant*: three tries and you were out, back in the fields. But a few students lingered for the fourth time around; they were known by less neutral-sounding names, like *idiot* and *voyou*.

The singing stopped. An expectant murmur stirred among the rows. The students were all looking toward the mango tree, where Aboï, clad in the functionary's synthetic pants and matching short-sleeved jacket, was emerging from the shade. In one hand he held a yard-long whip, two strips of lightly furred goatskin twisting around each other and ending in two tails; in the other, a sheet of paper. He walked out into the center of the field, burly chest upthrust, and addressed the students. It was the same bureaucrat's voice I remembered from the night of my arrival, and the same slightly dull peasant's face, with the front teeth protruding.

It seemed there had been a soccer game in which several of the older boys had gotten into fights. These fights were a blight on the esteemed reputation of the school, he said in his stiff French; they could not be permitted, nor go unpunished. The boys would be persuaded not to repeat them. He read a few names off his paper. From one of the rows, four boys about sixteen years old stepped out. Aboï approached them, grabbed a short, broad-shouldered boy by the collar, and yanked him forward. The boy put up his hands to cover his face, but he didn't shrink away or cry out when Aboï brought the whip down in four hard blows across his shoulders and arms. The snap of goatskin on flesh broke the morning silence and carried over to me, alone next to Aboï's office a hundred feet away. A few students gasped, others tittered. Aboï's face had come alive, it was wild-eyed and furious.

When the boy had taken the blows, he retreated back into the line and smiled weakly at his friends. The same punishment was delivered to the other three. A smaller boy cried out and limped back into line holding his thigh and turning an injured glare back at the principal. The others seemed to have a code of stoical silence. In line they shrugged at their classmates, shook their heads, made light of it.

When the offenders had been punished, Aboï went back to the middle of the field. No one made a sound. He read out another list of names, and his face and voice were neutral again, as if the violence of a moment ago had been unreal. These names were the *retardataires*, the latecomers. A sprinkling of students, about eight in all, slunk out from the rows and edged toward Aboï. He met them with his muscled arm raised. Fury had materialized again on his face: it looked real enough.

The goatskin whipped through the air and found flesh. *Snap!* A girl screamed and broke into frantic wails. The others abandoned their stoicism and scattered, and Aboï had to chase them, his whip raining down blows on whatever it could reach— backs, arms, buttocks. One little girl with gold hoops in her ears, who couldn't have been more than eleven, started to plead, "No monsieur—" *Snap!* The goatskin lashed across her arms. Aboï was hoarse with rage. "This will teach you to come on time!" She staggered off in tears. He had wheeled around to find the others, and his last lashes skimmed the khaki skirts of two girls scurrying away like beaten dogs.

He went back to the middle of the field. Within seconds the rubber-stamp voice had returned: assembly dismissed, everyone to class. The lines broke up and the students chatted their way across the field toward their classrooms. The teachers, who had been talking among themselves throughout the beatings, gathered their books and left the shade of the mango tree.

What unnerved me, even more than the hard lashes and the girls' screams, was the way Aboï switched his anger on and off. Every blow packed the force of rage, as if he were avenging the murder of a sister and not three minutes' tardiness. And then, before he'd caught his breath, he was the bureaucrat again. The beatings seemed a ritual, an addendum to the flag raising and anthem singing. The students looking on had treated the spectacle indifferently or as a joke. I wondered if this happened every morning. I wondered, too, if it was part of the curriculum Aboï had studied at the Ecole Normale Supérieure.

He was approaching me, casually trailing the whip down by his calf. "Monsieur Packer," he called out, smiling. "Welcome to CEG Lavié, Monsieur Packer. You permit me to call you Georges? Eh—" The smile broadened uncertainly. "Next time, please, Georges, attention during the national anthem. I noticed you were locking your moped while the children were singing. They might misinterpret you."

The image came before I could block it out: the vengeful shout, the arm raised, the snap of the whip across my shoulders.

My first day was not a success. Peace Corps had armed me, but not for this. In my bedroom I had a cardboard box full of pedagogy and six weeks of experience teaching practice classes in Atakpamé to a self-selected bunch of town kids, who came for the prizes handed out at summer's end and perhaps the oddity of a new shipment of white teachers—students who, in any case, wanted to be there. After each class, trainers and trainees would huddle and, on a scale of one to five, evaluate the day's lesson for voice, organization, body language, and use of blackboard.

I was well aware of my potential for irrelevance. In 1982 reports of drought and hunger were already trickling through obscure channels of information—repression in South Africa, massacre in Uganda, civil war in Angola—didn't lead me to conclude that the thing the continent needed most was a Renaissance studies major who could teach the relative pronoun. But the Togolese government seemed to consider American English teachers in its national interest and had already persuaded Peace Corps not to cancel the program once. My group would be the last. After us Peace Corps would limit itself to teacher-trainers, according to the philosophy in development circles of not duplicating and displacing local workers.

After a half hour at CEG Lavié I doubted I had the upper-body strength to duplicate or displace anyone. And I had already decided—or rather, I already knew, in my liberal bones—that I would not use corporal punishment in my classes. I clung to the vague idea that I might be able to earn my keep if I brought some of the values of my own education to receptive students in the classroom: independent thinking, self-motivation, love of learning. I hadn't come to spend two years with a whip in one hand and a pen in the other, demanding: "What's this? Repeat: It's a pen!"

And so, smiling and sweating and flushing green, I was led by Aboï into my four classrooms—floors deep in dirt, bamboo rafters exposed under metal roofs, a charcoal blackboard caked with so much chalk that it was ash gray, the bush just outside one wall and starting to come in through the window openings. In each class a boy slapped his hand on his desk as we entered, and forty or fifty children in khaki, sitting in pairs on benches at crude wooden desks, rose to attention. In each class Aboï informed the wide-eyed, whispering students that they were extremely fortunate at last to have their new American teacher, who was going to teach them correct English and whom they would respect—a tap of goatskin against his calf—as they did their other teachers. If there was any trouble I should report to him. In each class I delivered a thirty-minute speech I'd prepared in French on the benefits they would receive from learning English—the international language of commerce, the language of their neighbors, Ghana and Nigeria, the language written on cans of Quaker Oats and boxes of macaroni in the market; they would also have the chance to discover new cultures, a new world, new ways of thinking. . . .

Each class met me with the same blank, puzzled, or amused stares. My call for questions was answered with the same minute of silence. One boy ventured that he wanted to be a farmer when he grew up, and his classmates laughed and jeered; another, indicating my map, asked what the surface area of the

USA was and where my mother lived. My mother lived in California, I remembered that. The surface area of the USA? Was that square kilometers, or square miles? Well—I was an English teacher, not a geography teacher. Did he know the surface area of Togo?

"Fifty-six thousand square kilometers," answered a chorus of voices.

At noon, my button-down shirt wringing wet and my right hand covered with chalk as if I'd dipped it in a jar of flour, I rode the moped home for lunch, reflecting that perhaps I'd been a little too abstract and trying to remember what I'd come here to teach anyway.

"Good morning, Mistah Puckuh!"

"Good morning, class. How are you today?"

"I'm fine, thanks. And YOU?"

"I'm fine. Sit down, please. Who knows the date today?"

Hands shoot up. "I! I! I!"

"Yes? Adjo?"

Adjo, fourteen, the chief's niece, with high cheekbones and sidelong glances at her girl friends, slowly stands in the second row.

"Today—ees—Wesday—Novembah—threeth—1982."

"Any mistakes?"

"Oh, I, I!"

"Simkundu?"

Simkundu, an effeminate Kabyé boy with a mole above his lip, gets up confidently. "Novembah *thud*."

Adjo takes my chalk and goes to scratch the date across the blackboard.

For a year, sixteen classes a week started with this routine.

Difficulties surfaced fairly quickly. There was the problem of names. The Togolese teachers called students by their last names, but after a week of stumbling over the Agbodjavous, Amegawovors, and Kpetsus who proliferated in my classes, I broke custom (far from the last time) and went to first names. But here was the rub: among the Ewé your first name is determined by the day of the week you're born on. For example, a boy born on Wednesday is Kokou, a girl Aku; a boy born on Saturday is Kwamé, a girl Ama. So the pool of first names is severely limited, and in every class there were bound to be at least three or four of each name. In one class eight Koffis all sat in the same row. It was hard enough to keep the names straight, another problem altogether to get across which Koffi or Afi I wanted an answer from.

Then there were the copybooks. In the almost complete absence of textbooks, these lined notebooks became the students' lifelines. They also seemed to take the place of thinking. In their copybooks students wrote down with the care of medieval scribes every word their teacher deemed important enough to utter. Enter a mistake in one and it might never get corrected; lose one and a student might as well quit school. I once had to correct a geography teacher's exam. One of Kafui's questions was *"Qu'est-ce que le Nil?"* ("What is the Nile?") In response, every student wrote: *"Le Nil est loin des plus grands fleuves du monde"*—a piece of nonsense translating to "The Nile is far from the biggest rivers in the world." I had marked twenty-five answers wrong before I understood the mistake. The class had thought she had said *"loin des plus grands"* instead of *"l'un des plus grands"* ("one of the biggest . . .") and duly inscribed the mistake in their copybooks. The sentence had gone from mouth to copybook to exam like a defective product moving along an automated assembly line. Kafui laughed at the error, at the students' stupidity—but not at the system that wanted mimicry without thought. They should have listened better, she said.

But for two months I forbade copybooks. In training we'd learned to start with just spoken English, and it seemed a good idea. No English copybooks, then; and the kids responded like snails whose shells have been snatched off by a sadistic boy.

Finally, discipline.

One morning in November we were on the present progressive tense of the verb *to look at.* I walked up and down the columns of desks. "I'm *looking at* Afi. I'm *looking at* Kodjo. I'm *looking at* the window."

I had my fingers around my eyes like glasses, widening my eyeballs like a man possessed as I stared at Afi, Kodjo, the

window. They were in hysterics. Such moments teetered peril-
ously between good feeling and chaos. Aware of the risks, I still
felt I'd gained enough control over the class to try an experiment in putting on.

Suddenly a young boy on the left, sleepy-eyed and long-
necked, stood and shouted:

"Yovo, yovo, bonsoir!"

The laughter didn't die down, it was shut off in a second.
The boy, Kodjo, stood there as the smile dissolved on his face
and gave way to horror and disbelief. He was as stunned as
everyone else. He hadn't spoken the words, they had burst out
of him, a memory from early childhood, village talk, erupting in
the classroom; and in this setting they had the shock effect of
profanity. And yet he was right. I had been acting like a *yovo*,
which is to say exotic, bizarre compared with the other teachers
and their harsh or monotonous lectures—*akla*, Ama would have
said. I had broken the rules. Now anything went, and for an
instant Kodjo became a five-year-old again.

He was sinking back onto the bench, his mouth still half
open, his eyes weakly watching me. Gasps and murmurs rippled
across the classroom. I knew I would have to punish him. If I
didn't, the veneer of authority would crack even more and the
class might be lost for good. It had happened to the American
woman here before me. I wasn't going to let softness ruin a year
of teaching. Besides, I was furious, though I tried mightily not
to blow up. His name for me had triggered the vulnerable
anger that lay beneath the surface of even the most placid
African days. I ordered him to go outside and stand in the sun
for the rest of the class.

Fifteen minutes later Asamoa, the aging, bespectacled
Ghanaian English teacher, came by, whip in hand. He was
professeur de semaine this week, in charge of discipline. From the
doorway he motioned me over.

"Good morning, Mr. Packer. What has that boy over there
done?" He pointed with the whip at the transgressor standing
on the grass.

The truth had already embarrassed me enough. "He was
talking during the lesson."

"With your permission I would like to beat him."

"I've already punished him."

"But if he has misbehaved it is necessary to beat him. What will he learn otherwise?"

"He'll learn if you do?"

Asamoa stared at me as though I'd suggested his whip was made of Chinese silk. One part of me wanted nothing more than for the goatskin to deal a couple of blows and teach them all the lesson I wasn't willing to give; but with another part I knew it would make nonsense of what I was trying to do, of the way I'd been teaching a moment ago, of the way I wanted them to think of me. It would be cowardly too—yet another sign of my weakness. Asamoa relented and left, shaking his head.

When I went back into the room the students were whispering excitedly. We'd spoken in English, but they grasped the essentials. For most of them it must have been a revelation, the first time in their lives a teacher had intervened on a boy's behalf, and a boy who'd just insulted him too. It was plain that something decisive and irrevocable had happened. From that moment a handful of them probably began to think of me more as a friend than a *gendarme* and to associate the class with pleasure instead of pain. Students began appearing at my house with gifts of bananas or pineapples, and some of them learned English faster than I'd thought possible. But in that moment I knew that others—far more—wrote me off and my class. They would come every day, and even make an effort from time to time, but I had taken away the main incentive to learn. If I wasn't going to beat them, why should they bother?

Aboï came by to see me that night, on what he called a *"visite de courtoisie,"* showing that side of himself I associated with his degree from the Ecole Normale Supérieure and the elaborate words—*"corps professoral," "intervention collégiale"*— that swam to the surface of his conversation like water snakes. But he'd come to discuss something specific. Asamoa had spoken to him about the incident, and Aboï wanted to set me straight.

"Georges," he began with an uneasy smile, "you have an American idea about punishment. With your American students the soft method will work. But Africans are not self-disciplined; they need to be persuaded. Otherwise the students will perform badly in school and then their parents will say we of the teaching body are failing in our work. You see? It is an unpleasant duty. For the African, you need a stick. *Pour l'africain, il faut le baton.*"

I couldn't count the times I heard this argument. It was about the only thing Aboï and the teachers agreed on. "*Pour l'africain, il faut le baton*" should have been the motto of CEG Lavié, posted in bold letters over the doorway of Aboï's office. I only stopped hearing it when I'd exhausted myself asking. Sometimes the sentence came with a hint of sorrow, as if we were talking about a congenital ailment like sickle-cell anemia. Or else with scientific detachment, as an ethnography lesson. Or with a note of triumph: "*You* don't understand Africans; *we* do." Always it was uttered with the conviction of a law of nature. The only counterargument that produced a quiver of doubt was in effect an appeal to the same instinct: that beating students was against the law. The irony that the speaker, an educated adult, had to be included in this crew of lazy Africans seemed lost on everyone but me. We were always talking about someone else—them, the students.

A boy was whipped for correcting his teacher's definition of *archipelago*. Half a class was whipped for doing badly on a math test. Sometimes, as I heard a whipping through the cinder-block wall dividing my class from another, it sounded like a game. Kanyi, a good-looking young math teacher who wore Levi's and the latest shirts from France, seemed to whip girls as a way of flirting; his jokes and the laughter of the class were punctuated by the girls' screams. Nyaku, the soft-bellied music and Ewé teacher, had an unmistakable streak of sadism in him. When his turn to be *professeur de semaine* came around, he would rub his hands and giggle, "I'm going to tap them well this week."

Even when the goatskin wasn't used, it had a way of hanging in the air where a lesson was being taught. Teachers didn't deduce, or even lecture; they interrogated and commanded. "What is the penis?" I heard the biology teacher grilling his

6ième class one morning. *"What—is—the penis?* Yes, you?" A small boyish voice: "The penis . . . is . . . the reproductive organ . . . of males.. . ." The voice trailed off. From the front of the room: "No! No! Who knows? Nobody? The penis is *the reproductive and urinary organ of males which engorges with blood and achieves erection when stimulated!* You had all weekend to learn it. You're going to fail the exams if you go on like this. I'll repeat it." And the teacher repeated three or four times what the penis was, while forty twelve- and thirteen-year-olds frantically scribbled it word for word in their copybooks, next to their careful illustrations in several colors.

The biology teacher was named Koba. A skinny man with angular features and mirthful eyes, he came from a remote village on the northern end of the plateau, had just earned a degree in theory from the Ecole Normale Supérieure, and was now doing his *pratique.* In effect, he was under scrutiny and could be sacked at the end of the year if he didn't measure up. Like me, he was new in Lavié, new at teaching, and we became friends.

One morning after classes Koba invited me over for a lunch of *fufu.* He lived at the other end of the village from me, down a dirt trail that led off into cornfields and yam fields and then bush. His compound was a teachers' ghetto of modest concrete-and-iron buildings. A number of teachers lived there in relative isolation from the rest of the village. None of the teachers at the CEG came from Lavié; all had been assigned here by the government.

Koba's girl friend, an eighteen-year-old from his *3ième* class (officially, like the beatings, this was illegal), pounded *fufu,* while we sat in his cramped living room and drank warm beer fetched from the bistro by a student. Students were always running errands for teachers. One afternoon a week was set aside for TM, *Travail Manuel,* when whole classes had to bring water and firewood to teachers' houses.

"It isn't a good use of their time," Koba was saying, "but there is no alternative. We teachers are here on our own; we have no family in Lavié, and no time to do our own chores. So it's necessary for the children to do them."

"It must be hard, with your family so far away."

"Very hard, very hard! An African relies on his parents, his cousins. It's a nice thing to have a girl friend, but a girl friend isn't a sister. . . ."

His family also relied on him, he said. Of ten siblings he was the only literate one, the only functionary, and his salary had to be divided among a score of relatives back in Kouniohou ("Death Is Better"). He couldn't save a sou. "Things are difficult especially now, with the *crise économique*. Teachers haven't had a raise in three years. And some months I can't touch my salary at all. Since I'm a newcomer, they withhold it, to make sure I don't grab the money and quit the profession." A smile cracked his sharp features; his eyes danced ironically. "But it isn't like *chez vous*. We can't complain; we are silent."

As we dipped our fingers in the bowl of *fufu* the girl friend had brought in, Koba sketched a bleak picture of education in Togo. There was no money, everyone knew that; the national debt was even discussed in the newspaper. Fewer teachers could be hired, and as a result the degrees of those entering the job market meant less and less. Fifteen years ago a CEG degree was all you needed to teach in the CEG; it was all Asamoa had, for example. Ten years ago you needed a *bac*, from the *lycée*. Now it was an ENS degree, and already that was becoming worthless; soon a university degree wouldn't be enough. Koba himself was lucky to have slipped in before the gates closed.

"And the children see what is happening. They see that their older brothers and sisters with *bacs* can't get a job, and they see how hard it is even to get the *bac*. More and more of them flunk because there are fewer and fewer places available. The effect is a general demoralization. Our enrollment at CEG Lavié is declining. The boys go off to Kpalimé to learn carpentry or mechanics, or else they turn into *voyous*. It's a shame. The government tells us to return to the land. You've heard of *la révolution verte*. But who wants to work the fields after he's gone to school? We know what that work is like. It is painful. And today it doesn't pay either."

Then I quizzed him about the beatings. Did those help to make school desirable? He pondered, pinching off a morsel of *fufu.* He had given it a lot of thought, he said. At ENS a French instructor had taught them the new theories of child psychology, that one must treat the student as a person with a mind and a sense of dignity. It all sounded right. But now he was doing the *pratique,* and he'd found that *pratique* and theory had nothing to do with each other.

"When I started I tried to teach that way, and I had nothing but problems. The children don't learn. My effort is a drop in the ocean. I've already begun to change; I don't beat them, but I don't mind if somebody else does. You see, Georges, it is a thing we Africans learn at home. The mother and father teach respect and obedience with the back of their hand. By the time we go to school we are used to this, we couldn't learn any other way. It has to change in the family, where it starts."

I suggested that things never changed at home, that it was school that put new ideas in one's head.

He sighed. "I agree. We are at a crossroads. Many people want to change, but we don't quite know what to do. We can't liberalize now because behind us we have so many years of rigid discipline."

"But if—"

"That's how school began in Africa," he said, heating up. "The same way roads were built. The Europeans beat our fathers and forced them to go to school, just as they forced men to labor on the *route nationale.* We've always gone to school to the whip in Africa. The idea has been with us since colonization. That's why it's so difficult to change. You see?" He began to laugh. "It's your fault! And now the *yovos* come back here to tell us it was all a mistake, we have to start teaching another way!"

We both found this extremely funny. We laughed and laughed, and finished the *fufu,* and sent a student for two more bottles of beer.

I rode home to sleep the last hour of siesta before afternoon classes began. In the yard I found Atsu and Claudie having a play-fight. Atsu was chasing his younger brother, pretending to beat him with a stick. I asked what it was all about. Atsu pointed at Claudie and mocked:

"He doesn't know that six plus six makes twelve!"

George Packer

George Packer was born in Stanford, California and received his BA from Yale in 1982. His experience as a Peace Corps Volunteer, teaching English as a foreign language in rural Togo, is recounted in his first book, *The Village of Waiting* (1988 Random House), from which the story "Khaki and Goatskin" is excerpted.

Upon his return to the United States from Togo, Packer worked as a carpenter and writer in the Boston area. His short stories have appeared in the *Virginia Quarterly Review* and *Ploughshares*; his essays in *Wigwag, Dissent, Boston Review,* and *In These Times*; and his book reviews in *The Nation,* the *New York Times Book Review, Mother Jones,* and *Village Voice.*

Packer lives in the Boston area where he is a teacher of freshman English at Harvard University. He is a member of the Democratic Socialists of America and the National Writers Union. His current writing includes several essays on culture, class, and left-wing politics, as well as an essay on George Gissing. He has completed a novel, *The Half Man,* which will be published in the fall of 1991 by Random House.

ANCIENT SHELLS

Eileen Drew

When Ruzi told her about Bola, Miss Christina said that ugly English word she never explained in class and turned bright as hibiscus. Miss was always damp around the mouth and where her hair met her forehead, wet so the strands which didn't reach the knot behind fell like tiny snakes on her cheeks. When angry she was like hibiscus after rain.

"Miss Tomato," the students would say to each other, but Ruzi never saw her that color. Ruzi saw the skin so transparent that blue veins laced the hands, climbed the arms. Veins zigzagged across Miss's feet too, swelling, then flattening with each step as she passed Ruzi's desk. Back in tenth-grade biology, Citizen Emolo had said everyone's blood was blue inside and came out red, yet Ruzi still imagined Miss bleeding blue, like ink.

The first day of school, the new teacher had walked into the senior class trembling on thin spider legs. "Christina James," she wrote on the board, and then, "Benton, New Jersey, U. S. A." The letters were loopy, the lines slanted. Her French was funny but no one laughed; a teacher could punish. Missionaries hit and Africans made you kneel in the sun. Mrs. Baxter, Ruzi's second-grade teacher at the church school, had taught silence. Noisy people had their knuckles pounded with a ruler. One girl's finger was broken.

Miss Christina wasn't with a mission, though. "Volunteer" appeared on the board as she explained the one-year contract. Ruzi understood then that this white was a one-year missionary without a church. Run by the state, Kundu Girls' School had no religion.

Even more puzzling, this woman was single. Old Mrs. Baxter's husband had died, but Miss, with skin smooth as clay, was too young to be alone.

And why would anyone leave rich America?

"Why not?" was the answer, when Nzuzi up front asked. "Africa might have something better than money."

Not in the bush, not at Kundu. The town was so quiet teachers refused to come; they all worked in Bossiville. The principal still hadn't found a math and physics teacher for this year. What was there to do?—No music, no bars, no cinemas, no life. Nothing but a school.

"I like quiet," said Miss Christina. "It's clean."

Ruzi agreed, whites needed to slow down. The arm jerked across the blackboard, squeaking chalk. Pins were slipping from the knot of hair that looked crazy as a forest, with things hanging everywhere. If the hair were separated into eight parts, each knotted tightly to the scalp, Miss might be pretty. If she ate yams her face might get round, her nose less narrow. If she smiled.

Ruzi could braid beautifully. She'd learned on her mother and sisters, then her mother's friends and their daughters, fitting designs to each head's shape. She would memorize the newest Bossi styles on strangers in buses. Then, when Ruzi left the city for secondary school, her mother began going to the chic salons herself. Ruzi's technique became professional; each time she returned from Kundu for a holiday she could unravel the thread and pull apart the intricately woven tufts of her mother's stiff hair to redo the same style immediately on Mbengi, her sister. Mbengi strutted each experiment for days, refusing to carry anything on her head, until her mother yelled, "Lazy! Get away from the mirror and help Ruzi with the clothes. You're too pretty for your age."

Ruzi, though, would point to an empty stool on the patio

and tell Mbengi about Kundu while her sister sat watching. Laundry was Mbengi's chore now, but Ruzi was happy with her arms wet to the elbows, dipping cloth after cloth into pails of sudsy water. Her two smaller sisters always squeezed into Mbengi's patch of shade and listened too, eyes wide at Ruzi's stories of dormitory rats, or of the red, sticky, rainy-season mud.

"Is it like the village?" asked the youngest one.

"No. All the buildings are cement and there's electricity. It's school. I spend every morning in a classroom reading and writing, just like you will next year, except you'll come home every day. I wish I still did."

"Simon and Tuli like their school."

Her brothers were both smart. Even during vacations they read books, traded and then offered them to Ruzi, who laughed.

"They're boys," she said.

When her mother had told her she was going away to school, Ruzi had wailed, setting a pile of clean clothes on a kitchen chair. "I can stay here in Bossi, help you in the house," she said, wiping her eyes on the freshly folded sleeve of her father's shirt. "School isn't important for me, I'm barely passing."

Behind the stove her mother's face hung in steam. "Your father has decided. You will do better at Kundu with few distractions. He wants you to finish secondary school before you marry."

"For the dowry."

"For you also." The woody aroma of peanut stew somehow softened the voice. "Mintu wants an educated wife."

Folding the damp sleeve back on itself, Ruzi imagined the shirt was Mintu's, that school was finished and her father paid. They might live in a bush village after he finished studying agriculture at the university. Maybe even Abi village, where they'd met, where her father was born. According to him, Mintu would be a perfect husband, of a good clan from his own natal land. It was too early for arrangements, Mintu was still at secondary school, but everybody wanted them to marry. He wrote her letters. He visited when in Bossiville.

"But why can't I be educated here?"

"When do you study in this city? Already you think only of braiding hair. You'll get into trouble like all Bossi kids, drinking, dancing, smoking in the streets and missing school—stealing, even. You need discipline."

When Citizen Bola had said he'd raise her geography and history grades in exchange for evening meetings, his eyes tiny and dull as peppercorns had stung inside her stupid brain. Her last year was beginning badly, first the new white Miss and now this rat man. In the musty teachers' room Ruzi studied the few hairs on his pointy chin, the stick-out teeth and ears. Then the paint flaking off the wall around the bookshelves of faded texts. Maps were stacked against the one window; opposite, the door was open wide. Bola seemed to belong to the mildew smell of a room shut all summer. Would his house smell the same?

"You must come at night, carefully," he said.

The arrangement was familiar. Ruzi knew several girls— all very pretty—who passed classes this way. Too poor to pay dowry, many teachers were bachelors. Before Miss Christina, the first woman teacher Ruzi had known at Kundu, the students were the only single females. Ruzi said nothing. If she could think like a boy, she could pass her classes herself. Bola had said once last year that if he were God he never would have created women, because they couldn't think. The whole class had shouted, pointing at Tusamba and Povi with the highest marks, and he said, "Because they can memorize. You can memorize, but you can't think."

Now he was saying, "Last year you failed my courses. If you fail again this year you won't have the cumulative points to graduate. I want to help you, but after three years I can see you'll never learn my lessons."

He spoke like her father, hands clasped on the table. There were no questions; the conference ended when his hand waved her away. He knew she would come.

That night, she thought of Mintu as she walked without a storm lamp across the school grounds; she was sneaking through Abi to meet Mintu under the baobab tree. Inside Bola's salon lit by a bare bulb in the ceiling, she pictured Mintu in the rat man's place as they sat sipping palm wine. In bed it was easier because she closed her eyes, and the wine made everything just fuzzy enough for Ruzi to imagine Mintu's wide, slow hands. During the next day's history quiz, though, she remembered quick claws scratching.

Miss Christina didn't smile at first. The night her hair was down, she smiled. Ruzi was on her way to Bola's, an empty pail in each hand so if anyone asked she could be fetching water from the tap near his house, when she saw Miss. Perched on the concrete washing block in her yard, she was talking to her neighbors' children.

Hiding Miss's shoulders, arms, and most of her face, the hair was a magic veil grown from nowhere; certainly it couldn't all have come from the knot behind her head. As Ruzi neared she saw strands rising and falling in the breezy dusk. Otherwise so still, Miss was odd as an ancestor. Away from the classroom, she was smiling, oblivious to the children's fingers touching.

Ruzi crossed the lawn and put the buckets down. "Your hair is very long," she said.

"Yes, it's too hot to wear down during the day."

"Doesn't it itch?"

"No. At home I always wore it like this."

"*Go away!*" Ruzi shouted at the kids, who ran to a safe spot under a tree. "You don't have to let them bother you."

"It's something different for them. I don't mind."

Like the children, Ruzi had to touch. She took a clump in her hand and began braiding; clumsy in sudden softness, her fingers plunged as if through water. She wondered if Miss knew her from class. Would she guess where Ruzi was going?

"No one can see your face like this."

"Everyone knows who I am. It's getting dark anyway."

"In America, then. You shouldn't hide your face. It looks dirty, dangerous. An open face is prettier."

"I could shave my head." Smiling, Miss seemed to be joking. At the tip Ruzi let go so the braid unraveled itself. How would she fasten such straight, slippery hair? She answered, "That's what our men do when their fathers die. Shave their heads."

Miss Christina shook her hair behind her shoulders with a wild jerk like a tail swishing. At night, then, Miss was happy, not hard as a plate, or electric bright with sweat.

Picking up her pails, Ruzi said, "I must go before it's dark."

Bola had said she could come at twilight, with the pails for an excuse. Ruzi hated the black nights eerie with owls, bats, possible snakes.

People knew anyway, even after only two weeks. Girls in the dorm had noticed her bed empty every few nights and asked who, until she got the "B" on the history quiz. Then she told them rat stories, that Bola slept under his bed because he was afraid of light, that he nibbled at his sheets. In class they made holes in the papers he returned and held them up to each other to show he'd been hungry.

Miss Christina probably didn't know. She didn't know anyone's name in class yet.

The next day, serious again, she called on Ruzi by pointing the usual stubby finger.

Miss never hit. By the end of September, English class was crazy; if people weren't talking all at once they were napping, heads resting on folded arms. As long as they spoke English, Miss didn't care. "If you want to fail, go to sleep," she said. "If you want to learn, listen." They were studying the conditional.

Cheating was the crime she hated, and her punishment was sneaky. After Ruzi found the angry red zero on her composition she looked for Miss in the teachers' room. The dingy maps were spread all over now, leaning against chairs and table legs; they'd been coming to class with Citizen Bola. Whenever he set one up against the blackboard he pointed out all the countries with new names. That hard to label, the world seemed false to Ruzi. She could not imagine Miss Christina in the vast pale splotch that was America.

Seated at the table, chin in hands, Miss was staring at Asia. When she turned, Ruzi said, "Miss, you made an error."

"Let me see."

Miss concentrated on the paper, teeth shut hard. "You

cheated," she said finally.

Ruzi protested, although she had, in fact, copied the text from Mintu's book of fables. His school had used it his senior year and he'd said it might help. When Miss had told the class to write a fable, Ruzi had copied the one about Tarantula and Crocodile. Then she'd helped Mbonani, Nzuzi and Sanza by lending them the book. Helping was *good*.

Teachers didn't read homework. Ruzi was often returned papers with no marks but the grade at the top. Some teachers didn't even collect homework. So Ruzi had felt safe copying only the first two paragraphs from the text even though the fable went on four more pages. She figured she couldn't do worse if she wrote her own English.

But zero!

"I warned you," said the teacher. "If you cheat, you get zero." Ruzi remembered the word *warn* from a recent lesson. On the board Miss Christina had drawn a palm tree with all the fronds blown in one direction, squiggly lines for the wind, and then two people outside a hut with a thatch roof. The word *good-bye* hung in a bubble like a cloud over the boy, while the girl pointed at the fronds.

Miss had turned to ask who the girl was and everybody knew; she appeared regularly on the board with the new vocabulary words. "Lolo!" the class chorused. And who was the other? "Tuli," they shouted, "her friend!" Everyone clapped, the drawings with Tuli and Lolo together were best because they were getting married.

"One person," said Miss, holding up one finger so the class would not answer all at once. "What is Tuli doing?"

Sanza in the front raised her hand. "He is leaving."

Yes, he was saying good-bye. The class explained, student by student, with last week's vocabulary, that Lolo was looking at the *wind* and that a *storm* was coming. "Don't go!" was what she said to Tuli.

Then Miss began to draw again. In the new picture Tuli was on the road by himself under a big cloud, a real one this time with a crooked line for lightning in it instead of words. Rain slanted down from the cloud; Tuli dripped.

"Is Tuli happy?" Miss asked. Palms drummed on desks: No! Intelligent? No! Was he surprised? (And there Miss shaped an "O" with her lips.) No. Why not? Because Lolo *warned* him.

They went around the class making sentences with the new word, *warn*. Ruzi had said, "I warn you about boys," and everyone had laughed, even Miss.

Now Miss was sober as she handed the failed composition back to Ruzi in the teachers' room. "I warned you," she repeated. Then, "I have the same book."

"No. Not cheating." Ruzi tried to look injured, but Miss told her to leave.

At the door, she saw the girls filing back into classrooms, a layer of white shirts above blue skirts sucked inside the building.

"Ruzi!" she heard.

Miss had learned her name.

Funny French replaced the slow English. "Ruzi, you don't need to cheat. Come for tutoring. Come in the afternoon."

She didn't have to, but she went, twice each week. First just to see, then she didn't know why. Other girls went, too; sometimes Ruzi had to wait, flipping the pages of her notebook, because Miss explained each person's problem alone. At the dining table Ruzi watched the blunt fingers write out sentences, lists and charts. Saying words was easier than writing them. Even in French, Ruzi had trouble putting her thoughts on paper. In her letters to Mintu, Bola never seemed to fit.

After lessons, Miss would show photographs of America, some very white with snow where people looked fat in thick clothes. She played tapes of American jazz, which sounded full of air. Ruzi scanned the room for foreign things, made Miss explain the battery recharger, the vitamins, the insect repellant which smelled so bad. Miss had no American perfume or cosmetics, she said. She didn't seem to like them.

Visitors were always knocking, if not students, then teachers whom Miss asked to come back later. "Come this evening, I have beer," she would say, "We'll play cards." A truck merchant brought her a case every few weeks, but instead of selling bottles she invited men to share. Twice at dawn, returning to the dorm from Bola's, Ruzi saw men leaving. One she knew from his antelope walk: the seventh-grade teacher. The other she was too far away to tell.

Wives never visited, but the children from next door came banging, buckets in hand, whenever their cistern was empty. Then Ruzi missed her family, imagined her own little sisters spilling water the way these kids did as they picked up the pails that Miss placed on the floor by the kitchen sink. Ruzi wanted little heads to braid.

When she was not at Miss Christina's or Bola's, Ruzi spent her free time braiding hair. Afternoons, the girls practiced on each other, grouped in pairs on straw mats under the mango tree. Ruzi braided best, twisting beads and colored thread inside loops that never fell. Relaxed in old rapas tied loosely so they could sit on their heels, they all told everything, what they knew and what they'd heard, whose lover was best. Ruzi talked about Mintu, meeting him at Abi when they were both visiting relatives; she'd been only twelve the first time, hadn't even worn lipstick! They'd been waiting so long to marry because of silly school; would her father make them wait until the full dowry was paid? Mintu wouldn't have money until he finished studying, for two whole years. Ruzi paraphrased his letters, the parts about how beautiful she was, and her friends laughed and sighed, but then they worried with her that he'd fall in love with someone else and marry against tradition.

By December Ruzi had filled three copybooks with English notes where her own delicate handwriting alternated with Miss Christina's scrawl. The teacher bit her lip as she wrote, crouching over the pen so her back arched unnaturally. Yet each time she lifted the pen and looked up, shoving the book towards Ruzi, she smiled, pulling damp strands of hair away from her eyes. When Ruzi told her about Mintu she smiled, too, until Ruzi asked who *she* would marry. Miss said she wanted to work and travel, not marry, and when Ruzi kept asking questions the white face got pink the way it did in class when Miss was about to shout.

Ruzi never laughed, although in class everyone else would

each time Miss stood turning color, the corners of her mouth wiggling like the tips of leaves in the smallest wind. Miss was funniest when she shouted. Once when Nzuzi stole her roll book she exploded, her English sentences strung together like the cars of a fast train.

At school she was angry more and more, slamming her books together before she left class even when the girls were trying to understand. But her lessons were strange; she rarely used the stories in the grammar book. Instead she brought dittoed texts about current events like overpopulation, or what to feed babies, or about wars in countries whose names Ruzi never remembered. All were written by Miss in English; Ruzi would hear the typewriter drumming as she arrived for tutoring, saying to herself new words like *ambush* or *lactate*. Lolo and Tuli were married with three children, but no longer liked each other. Miss had taught *divorce*.

In some ways, Miss Christina was like Mrs. Baxter. But instead of God, Miss talked about birth and death. Both women wanted to change Tambala. Miss wanted to so badly that when the girls couldn't learn, her own mind broke. When she said they should have few children, Tusamba told her she was wrong, that for parents children were money, and that Tambala was all empty space anyway. The rest of the class cheered, the hibiscus face perspired, everyone laughed, and Miss let out her ugly word.

Ruzi noticed that Miss used it often in its own paragraph, if that's what a paragraph meant, alone with lots of silence. In French films Ruzi had seen angry whites shouting words about the body or death, sometimes at no one. Tambalan had those words, but only for calm talking.

Miss needed quiet hands in her waterfall hair. Ruzi's knots, though, were meant for dense tufts close to the scalp; on Miss they wouldn't hold. Ruzi thought she could fix Miss's nails instead. Before the midyear vacation, the last time Ruzi went for tutoring, she promised to bring Miss some nail polish. She formed the English words, "Then you will be pretty. Then you will be happy."

Miss had put her hands under the table, in her lap. "I'm

happy, Ruzi."

"No children. No husband."

Miss brought out her hands and lay them flat on the wood. The nails didn't grow beyond the skin at all, and a few fingers were scraped raw at the tips. White fingers looked weak, painful.

"Very small." Ruzi pointed at a nail.

"I bite them."

That puzzled Ruzi, even when Miss explained in French that it was a nervous habit. Quietly, she added, "I don't think Tambalans have nervous habits."

Ruzi's fingers were slender and competent. Braiding, they twisted back and forth, back and forth like village dancers to drums. Her shiny nails worked like a comb, her palms pressed the tufts flat.

Home for the holidays, she had found her mother dressed as usual in billows of pastel fabric. Sometimes it was silk from France. Mostly she was draped in cotton as she moved through the house, in and out of rooms, down halls, up stairs so gently Ruzi never heard her. As Ruzi was unpacking the day she arrived, her mother commanded, "Come and braid my hair."

Ruzi turned to see her heavy figure in the hall, bare toes visible beneath the curtain of her skirt. When Ruzi had first said hello she'd noticed the hair, knotted into rows with small shells woven in, curving in parallel lines from temples to spine.

"Can we keep the shells?"

"They're for you."

They sat in the courtyard where her sisters were cleaning fish. Mbengi grinned, waiting her turn. "I'll be beautiful," she said.

The shells were tiny inward-curling things, with speckles of brown and red. You found them sometimes at the ocean; they were rare in Bossi. Mostly they remained from when they had been used for money in ancient times. They were like little tough-skinned flowers, Ruzi thought, unthreading them one by one from her mother's hair. Mbengi would wear them next, then Ruzi herself would wear them back to school.

"Lutete has spoken to your father," said Ruzi's mother.

Lutete was Mintu's father. That meant marriage plans. Ruzi's fingers felt like someone else's.

"For when?" she asked.

"When you finish school. Your father will accept a first gift and wait for the rest until Mintu can pay. Mintu is coming Friday to present the gift."

Ruzi was at the end of a complicated knot but she let go to hug her mother, then her sisters. "And I thought Papa was greedy!" She held the youngest by the shoulders. "You have a fine Papa," she said.

When Ruzi finished braiding the shells into Mbengi's hair the rows were uneven, the knots bumpy. "You weren't sitting still," she accused, and Mbengi answered, "Is this how you'll do your children?" But they were laughing.

Mintu arrived Friday in a taxi and lugged to the door a case of bottles. Instead of palm wine or beer, he brought American whiskey. Ruzi's father didn't drink much, but he nodded with excitement because he could sell bottles. Only as they sat for the conference did he stop shaking Mintu's hand. Then he waved everyone away, ordering Ruzi's mother to bring glasses. After a while Ruzi's brothers were invited to join them with two more glasses, and finally the women were admitted to the salon where the men were settled deep into cushions on the chairs. A ceremonial toast was poured, even a few drops for each younger girl, and when the congratulations were fading Ruzi asked Mintu to come outside.

"Why haven't you written me?" he asked as they found stools on the patio.

"What would happen if I didn't pass this year?"

"Are you failing?"

"I will unless you talk to my teacher. He'll leave me alone if he believes I'm getting married."

"What?"

"It's an arrangement," Ruzi said, deep and fast so it sounded hateful as crazy white words. She waited, and felt Mintu's hand around hers tense up. He was good. He'd be angry, but not at her.

Mintu whispered, "Were you doing so badly? Is that why you didn't write? You should have told me."

Ruzi tried to find stars, but the glare of the city filmed over the sky. Kundu had so many stars.

"I'm sorry," she said. "I didn't know what to do. If I failed, we would have had to wait longer. You might have stopped waiting."

"Do you like him?"

"He's a rat," she said, and started to cry. His arms went around her, the solid night arms she'd created out of Bola time after time.

"I'm going to Kundu tomorrow. He won't bother you again."

She wiped her nose on the hem of her rapa; she'd change it when she went inside. Mintu leaned away; she felt him trying to see her. Of him she saw only outlines: hair, nose, jaw. Hard, broad jaw.

Ruzi returned to school with the nail polish. When she asked Miss Christina the first day back if she could come that afternoon, Miss laughed, holding up her stubby nails, but said yes anyway. Miss laughed all through her lesson as students made sentences about Christmas and New Year's. Miss was happy. With blue chalk she drew water, where she'd gone. Copying down the word _ocean_, Ruzi wondered if Miss was happy to be back at Kundu, or to have left. Maybe she'd been with a man. Maybe she was getting married, too.

They sat outside on Ruzi's straw mat that she had brought rolled and balanced on one shoulder. No English books today; this visit was special. As they settled, Miss crosslegged and Ruzi sitting on ankles, Ruzi told the news. She punctuated her French with the percussion of tiny balls inside as she shook the bottle of polish. Like a calabash.

"Congratulations," Miss nodded, looking pleased as her nail turned red as a tomato. Her skin, too, was dabbed red at the tip.

"My fiancé studies agriculture, he's going to work for the state."

"And what will you do?"

"Children, Miss. And I can braid hair for extra money, while Mintu is in school."

Miss swallowed.

Ruzi started on the third nail. She wanted to ask about Miss's men, and began with, "You need a husband, Miss."

"You're wrong."

Ruzi tried to explain. Married, women mattered.

"Your English is so good now. Doesn't school matter?"

Ruzi's brush hovered over the pinkie. Now she was angry. If she were white, she thought, she'd be red as the polish. "I'll tell you about school. Girls go to school so bachelor teachers don't have to get married! We go to school so our dowries will be high, so our fathers will be rich. And since we can't marry until we finish, there's nothing to stop teachers like Bola!"

"Bola?"

Ruzi realized that Miss hadn't known. After smearing polish on the pinkie, she dropped the hand. What could this stranger understand about happiness? Miss was not intelligent enough to be a teacher.

Ruzi told her about the arrangement and Miss went hibiscus color, spitting out the ugly word.

Ruzi said, "Give me your other hand, I will finish."

However, Miss was unfolding, rising, slipping her feet into thongs.

"Miss, you can't leave, we've only done one hand. Come sit down, it won't take long." One hand of red nails and one of white was grotesque, like a cripple.

"If you were less worried about nails you wouldn't have this problem with Bola."

"But it's over, it's fixed!"

Miss Christina didn't hear, she'd already slammed her door. Ruzi thought of the hollow rattle of hinges that echoed at school each time Miss ran home, angry at everyone laughing, mid-lesson. They would crowd the classroom windows, listening. They wondered if she cried.

The next day everyone whispered about the five red nails;

what did they mean? Muslims grew the nails on their little fingers long enough to curl like horns. Maybe in America people without churches painted their nails like Miss.

Ruzi didn't tell.

When Miss called on her, the pale eyes saw something secret, like when Miss had looked at Asia. Although Ruzi's answers were correct, Miss didn't smile. No smile, no red. A ghost face.

That afternoon was Tuesday, Ruzi's tutoring day, but when she knocked at Miss Christina's door no one answered. As Ruzi returned to the dormitory, avoiding mangoes fallen from the trees, she saw Miss striding fast at the end of the avenue, skirt swishing. The principal lived over there.

Ruzi joined the girls braiding and offered the shells from her mother's hair. Tusamba wanted them, so Ruzi sat behind her, combing out the old braids. She told the story of Mintu's visit to Kundu. He'd spoken only to Bola. Mintu was tall with muscles tough from working outside; all he'd had to do was warn the little rat, and Bola had promised to give Ruzi "Bs" at the end of the year. That morning in the hall, Bola had actually congratulated her.

Ruzi was beginning to braid when Miss came thudding up the road.

She was redder than ever, "like the sun before it disappears," said Tusamba.

The road was sticky from the morning rain, and a thick layer of mud covered Miss's thongs. Only Ruzi knew why she was angry. Whites always got angry about sex. The principal had probably been polite, but he wouldn't care; he had his own way of helping. For money he would change student records.

When Miss Christina was alongside the girls, she stopped, mismatched hands on hips.

"Good evening, Miss," they chorused in English.

Her French came out like thunder. "Why are you girls always playing with hair? Every afternoon you're out here giggling like idiots, trying to make yourselves beautiful, and for what? So your men will think you're good enough to treat like animals!"

Tusamba straightened. "We're not animals."

"Then stop acting like them."

As Miss started towards her house, Ruzi could see the specks of mud on the backs of her legs. Whites didn't know how to walk slowly. Tambalan women knew to lift heels from mud carefully. Laughing with everyone else, Ruzi was sad. How sad that Miss had no friends, did not even want any. Men were all she had. No one to fix her hair or nails. What did white women talk about? Were they all so worried, reading and writing? Didn't they gossip, sing, touch? Miss's hand had felt cold, sick; Ruzi couldn't hold it again.

Eileen Drew

The daughter of a Foreign Service officer, Eileen Drew was born in Casablanca, Morocco and moved every few years according to her father's assignments. Her early memories of Morocco and Nigeria are hazy, but from the time she arrived as a third-grader in Guinea, through the years she spent in Ghana, and then later as a Peace Corps teacher in Zaire, her consciousness has been profoundly imprinted by Africa. In addition to her years of living and traveling in Africa, Drew has lived and studied in Korea.

Drew received a BA from the University of California, Santa Cruz in 1979, and an MFA in creative writing from the University of Arizona in 1986. She was also a Scholar at the Bread Loaf Writers' Conference in Middlebury, Vermont, in 1987. Her stories have appeared in *Triquarterly*, *Antioch Review*, *Black Warrior Review*, *Nimrod*, *Literary Review*, and *Sonora Review*.

In 1985, Drew was awarded the *Nimrod* Katherine Anne Porter Prize; in 1987, *The Literary Review* Charles Angoff Award; in 1987-88, the *Black Warrior Review* Literary Award; and in 1988, she was a finalist for the Drue Heinz Literature Prize. In 1989, she won the Milkweed National Fiction Award for *Blue Taxis: Stories About Africa* (1989 Milkweed Editions) a collection of short stories, in which "Ancient Shells" first appeared.

Drew lives with her husband, Lance Rosedale, in northern California, where she was recently a coordinator at the Lao Family Community, Inc. in Richmond. She currently teaches English as a second language at the Mt. Diablo Adult School in Concord and is at work on new fiction.

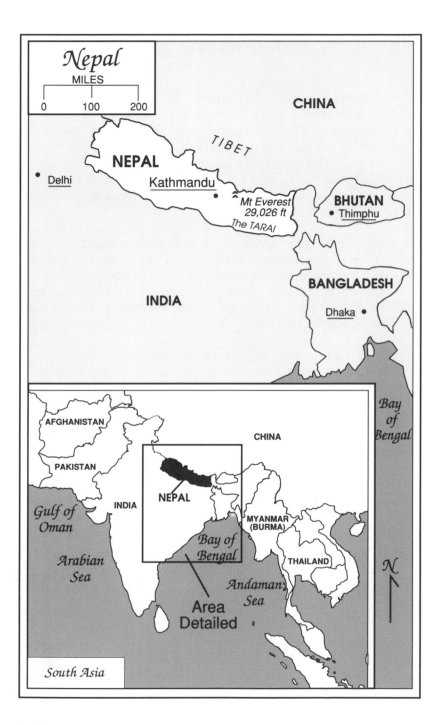

THE BRAVE OOARRIOR

Barbara Kerley

Head Sir, the headmaster of the school, stands six feet tall and 200 pounds, a giant by Nepali standards. Beside him, his friend Shastri, short and fat, looks like a younger brother who wants to tag along. Shastri is pigeon-toed, which accentuates his fatness. When he enters a home he steps out of his thongs and they remain, toed-in together, on the ground outside.

Shastri is the more learned of the two. He is the scholar of religion, the sustainer of culture for future generations. All teachers are respected in the village, but Shastri is revered for his extensive knowledge of Hinduism. He does more than teach: he performs weddings, blesses new houses and shops, and leads the villagers in prayer during the many Hindu festivals. Head Sir is more politically minded.

Head Sir teaches geography, barking lectures at the students, assigning them to read aloud from the textbook. He has one frayed map of the world, printed in the fifties. It ignores recent history, disregarding the birth of African nations, leaving whole the Asian nations which war has torn asunder. On Head Sir's map the world is static.

Shastri's subject is more dynamic by far. The myriad Hindu gods have myriad incarnations, with a name and a myth to be taught for each. Shastri spends the entire year of his seventh grade class teaching the incarnations of Lord Shiva. He repeats the lessons in tenth grade.

"The Hindu triumvirate is composed of Brahma, Vishnu, and Shiva," he explains. "Who is Brahma?"

"The Creator," his students respond.

"Who is Vishnu?"

"The Preserver."

"Who is Shiva?"

"The Destroyer and Recreator."

Seventh graders learn from Head Sir that the Himalayas, just in view to the north, contain the world's tallest mountain. Mount Everest, 29,028 feet tall, lies on Nepal's northern border.

"How tall is that in meters?"

"Eight thousand, eight hundred and fifty-three point five meters."

"And what nation is to the north of Mount Everest?"

"Tibet."

"Ah, yes, Tibet," Head Sir nods, switching to English. "Tibet is a very cold place."

But the seventh graders also learn that Mount Kailas lies in the Himalayas. Lord Shiva's sacred home is on Mount Kailas. Lord Shiva retires to Mount Kailas to meditate under a tree, denying himself all earthly pleasures.

"Head Sir," the students ask in geography class, "where is Mount Kailas?"

"Mount Kailas?"

"Yes, sir. Lord Shiva's home, where he is worshipped by the gods and seers."

"Ah, yes. Mount Kailas," Head Sir nods. "It is here," he gestures vaguely at the little bumps on the map. "In the Himalayas. In Tibet."

"Where is his tree?"

Head Sir frowns. "His tree?"

"Yes, sir. Lord Shiva's tree, where he meditates."

"Ah yes, his tree," Head Sir says.

"Is it at the top of Mount Kailas?" a student asks.

"Which direction does Lord Shiva face when he meditates?" another adds.

"He doesn't face any direction," the first student says. "He can see in all directions at once."

"Maybe he closes his eyes when he meditates," another says.

"He looks at the sun. Just like Shastri *ji* does when he says his prayers."

"Where is Lord Shiva's tree, sir?" the first student asks again.

"It is there, on Mount Kailas," Head Sir says quickly. "Ask Shastri just where."

By the time the seventh graders are tenth graders, they have learned to separate these realms of knowledge. They do not ask Head Sir where Shiva's tree is, nor Shastri, Mount Kailas' elevation.

Head Sir likes to practice his English, although few people in the village understand it. English is a status symbol; it sounds important. He has bought a book of *Useful English Phrases* which he reads in the school office and sometimes to his students if he has no lesson prepared. The book was printed in India, but is sold in Nepal as well. Head Sir memorizes Chapter Seven, "Merchants and Shop Talk."

"That turban sits very ooell on you," he reads. Like most Nepalis he cannot pronounce the sound 'w'. "That **turban** sits very ooell on you. That turban sits **very** ooell on you." The book includes intonation practice, but there is always room for improvisation. "That turban sits very ooell **on** you."

Shastri knows but a little English. Like most English learners, he first acquired his 'ings'. Unlike most, however, Shastri has never progressed further.

"The man is talking there," he says of Head Sir, nodding in pride. "The man is talking **English** there!"

Head Sir lives alone in the village. His family lives in the Tarai, the hot lowland which borders India. He returns to his family for festivals, walking four hours down the steep hillside. The road is littered with rocks and all of them move. The descent is a rutted, dusty, drunken slide. The trip back up is a hot steady exercise akin to climbing stairs for six hours. Head Sir's wife runs the family farm and looks after the children. Head Sir earns a moderate monthly paycheck and small political advantage.

"There's no place like home, eh Shastri *ji*?" Head Sir muses, pointedly recalling "Hearth and Home," Chapter Two. "Home is ooere the heart is." Head Sir loves to be reflective in English.

Shastri giggles. He rarely understands what Head Sir says, but it is English. They walk toward the bazaar. "The dog is sleeping there," Shastri responds, pointing. "The dog is sleeping long time." Head Sir would not admit it, but Shastri's popularity is good for his own image. They will wander the bazaar all afternoon, Shastri ministering to the community, Head Sir maintaining influence through visibility. But first the two men stop at Shastri's house. Shastri's wife will make them a snack.

"A oooman's ooork is never done, eh Shastri?" Head Sir nudges conspiratorially.

"My house," Shastri says, happy to be home.

Shastri's house is in the village. He has several children whom he tousles on the head in a vague, ineffectual manner, his affection diffused by his role as father of the community. His wife runs the household and disciplines the children. She cooks well and plentifully for Shastri, spreading clarified butter on his *rotis*, frying spicy potatoes to munch on after school. Shastri is also fed at every festival and is frequently invited to share a cup of tea.

"You've arrived?" Shastri's wife says in familiar greeting. "Please sit down," she says to Head Sir. She smiles at her husband and leaves to prepare a snack.

From corners and rooms Shastri's younger children appear, happy fat toddlers, three or four of them. They jump on Shastri, avoid Head Sir altogether.

"A man is king of his castle," Head Sir comments, quoting the book. "No man is an island," he adds. "Eh Shastri," he asks in Nepali. "In your own home you are like a king, isn't it so?"

Shastri shakes his head, laughing nervously. "No. No. I am not the king. The king is in the kitchen."

"A man is king of his castle, but a oooman is master of his heart." Chapter Four, "Love and Marriage."

Shastri and Head Sir wander the bazaar together, the giant

and the mouse. Many of the villagers do not like Head Sir. He is pompous and dominating. But if the villagers want to chat with Shastri, Head Sir is there, too. Thus Head Sir also gets many afternoon snacks.

"Ah, yes," Head Sir says, surveying the bazaar. "The picturesque bazaar." He does not know what 'picturesque' means, but it is in Chapter Six.

"The oooman is standing there," Shastri points out.

"Yes," Head Sir nods. "The humble villagers are happy in their daily chores."

Shastri giggles with embarrassed pride, forming large dimples in each cheek.

"Shastri *ji*, please come. Please sit down." A woman motions to Shastri, inviting him to her house. Head Sir comes along. The house is made of mud. The roof is thatched. Shastri sits down on the stoop in front of the house, a mud platform which extends out from the wall. "Sit down, rest yourself," she says. Head Sir sits down with a large sigh.

Shastri is beaming with pleasure. Two little girls, the woman's daughters, peek out at him from the house. "Come. Come here," he waves to them.

The woman stands up. "Please have some tea," she offers Shastri.

Shastri shakes his head. "No need. No need. I've **just** had some."

"But have some now." She hustles into the kitchen.

"Come," Shastri says to the smallest girl. "What's your name?"

"Sushila," she peeps.

Shastri giggles delightedly. "Sushila. And what's your sister's name?"

By the time the woman returns with the tea, both girls are standing next to Shastri. He is showing them a finger game. "Fish! Fish! Fish!" he says, wiggling his index finger. He shows the smallest girl how to make her tiny finger a fish. "Frog!" he cries, clamping her finger with his thumb.

The girls shriek with laughter, running away. In a minute they are back. "Play again," they command breathlessly.

"Please have some tea." The woman gives Shastri a glass of tea, rich and milky. She gives a glass to Head Sir. "Please drink." Next to the men she places a plate of *pakodas*, fried vegetable snacks.

"Ah, *pakodas*." Head Sir eats robustly, smacking the oily salt off his fingers. The woman stands and watches. "Is there any *raksi*?" Head Sir burps. He has a reputation for drinking heavily.

The woman frowns and shrugs, disappearing into the kitchen. She returns with a bottle, but only one glass. She knows that Shastri will not drink alcohol; he is a strict Brahmin. He is a priest. She pours a glass for Head Sir, hesitates, then places the bottle beside him.

"How is your family?" Shastri asks the woman.

The woman nods. "Fine."

"Brothers . . . aunts and uncles?"

"Everyone is fine."

"Your mother has been ill, hasn't she?" Shastri asks with concern. Other villagers keep him informed. News is passed along in the teashops, on the road, at the water tap.

The woman shrugs. "She is old."

Head Sir burps loudly, pouring himself a second glass of *raksi*. His belly is full and the *raksi* warms his insides. "A feast for the eyes," he says, burping. "My eyes are bigger than my stomach."

Shastri and Head Sir walk over to the clearing by the pond. It is being prepared as a large campsite. The Minister of Transportation is coming through town. He will ride a horse up the mountain roads, stopping in the village for the evening. Head Sir is excited. He talks about the Minister's impending arrival with the Mayor and the owner of the largest shop in the village. They congregate at the site, making plans.

"A goat will be cut," the Mayor says. "My best goat. We will let the Minister see how beautiful it is before we cut it."

"We must have *raksi*," Head Sir points out. "Lots of *raksi*."

"Of course," Lal says. "But hidden. The Minister may not drink in public. He may say he doesn't drink. We'll store the *raksi* in my shop until nightfall."

"My best goat," the Mayor continues. "And Shastri will say a prayer before the sacrifice, eh Shastri?"

"Yes," Shastri nods. His dimples appear.

"That goat weighs sixty pounds," the Mayor says.

"What about *tarkari*?" Lal asks. "Even my shop cannot get vegetables. Only potatoes are sold in the bazaar."

"I will tell the students to bring vegetables from their home gardens," Head Sir says. "That will be **my** contribution to the feast."

The men inspect the campsite, looking for stones. Head Sir is concerned about the dust. He sends a worker to the pond again and again for water to dampen the ground. Shastri goes home to dinner. Head Sir stays, talking importantly with the Mayor, watching the young women pass by on the road. He eats dinner in a teashop after dark.

Head Sir frequently goes to Shastri's house after dinner and invites him to wander the bazaar again. Tonight they go to Lal's shop, still open and dimly lit. A small brass lamp burns oil, leaving a sooty black residue on the lamp glass.

Lal offers Head Sir a cigarette. They smoke together, knocking the cigarette ash deftly on the floor. In the morning Lal's wife will sweep the ash away. Lal offers a piece of cinnamon bark, spicy and slightly sweet, to Shastri. Shastri moves the cinnamon around on his tongue. It burns if left in one place too long.

"We should ask the Minister for money," Head Sir says.

"Yes," Lal agrees.

"For the school."

"Yes."

But Head Sir is thinking about more personal gains. A move to the District Education Office, twenty miles but years away. A move to the Department of Education in Kathmandu. A move to the Department of Transportation. It doesn't matter.

Lal pulls a bottle of *raksi* out from behind the shelves. He yells for his wife, for two glasses and a cup of tea for Shastri. She scowls. It is late and there is no milk.

"No need. No need," Shastri protests. "I **just** ate." He rubs his tummy to demonstrate.

But Lal sends his wife away and she returns momentarily with the glasses. "It is black tea," she apologizes to Shastri. "There is no milk."

"Not to worry," Shastri replies.

"A gracious host serves his guests and his god," Head Sir quotes from the book. "Hospitality is next to cleanliness. Is next to godliness, eh, Shastri?"

"The two men is drinking there. Drinking *raksi* there," Shastri notes.

"I'm going home," Lal's wife says.

"All that glitters is not gold," Head Sir says, contentedly stretching back with his glass. "Eh, Shastri? All that glitters is not gold."

Shastri giggles.

"Please excuse my wife," Lal says, ignoring the English. "She is not feeling well."

"Spare the rod and spoil the child," Head sir suggests. "Women must be beaten," he adds in Nepali. Lal agrees. "Do you beat your wife?" Head Sir, filling his glass, asks Shastri.

"No. If I'm not careful she beats me."

Head Sir guffaws and he and Lal are laughing. Shastri giggles with them, happy to have made a joke. The men share two bottles while Shastri dozes off in the corner. Head Sir wakes him later. When he stays out late, Shastri sleeps in Head Sir's *deraa*, a room above the shop. The men climb onto Head Sir's mattress and Head Sir falls asleep, snoring drunkenly, drooling slightly. His head flops against Shastri's shoulder.

School is cancelled on the day of the Minister's arrival. Head Sir orders the children to bring vegetables from their gardens. The eggplant, spinach and beans pile up on the table in the school office. He sends the children out to get flowers. They will make flower *maalas* to place around the Minister's neck when he arrives. Head Sir leaves for the camp site, ordering the school *peon* to bring the vegetables over in the afternoon. He gives the *peon* a *rupee* to buy onions and garlic. "Bring these, too," he instructs.

The Mayor has brought his beautiful goat, a large brown creature obliviously grazing on the small plants by the edge of the site. Lal donates firewood, sending his wife to the forest to get more. She departs, scowling. She will return in several hours, carrying a large bundle of wood on her back. The men stand around supervising the preparations. Vegetables are brought from the school by the *peon* and several older boys. The girls bring flower *maalas* strung from marigolds.

The porters for the Minister's party arrive several hours before he does. They have walked since dawn, loaded down with equipment in large triangular baskets on their backs. They stop at the campsite, muscular and gaunt. They pull *bidis*, coarse local cigarettes, out of their pockets and rest in the shade. Then they pitch a huge tarp like an open tent. It shades the site but allows the breeze to pass through. Chairs and a table are brought out from the police station, a wooden cot is commandeered for the Minister from above the teashop.

Head Sir's excitement mounts. He supervises activities he knows nothing about. He tells the porters how to pitch the tarp, instructs the teashop proprietress on the way to make curry. Head Sir paces the bazaar, doggedly pursued by Shastri with pigeon-toed persistence. "You is ooalking there," Shastri says. Head Sir paces until late afternoon, until the Minister's white horse is seen on the crest of the road. Head Sir clears his throat and spits. He prepares to meet the Minister.

There are introductions and solicitations about the trip. The children welcome the Minister, placing flower *maalas* round his neck. The Minister's horse is attended to. The Minister is offered tea, snacks, meals, *raksi*, a nap, a cigarette and a trip to the water tap to bathe. But the Minister wants a drink of water and a tour of the town. "I have been sitting on this horse all day," he jokes, rubbing his behind. "I want to walk." The Minister's joke is uproarious, and the Mayor is pleased to note that the horse is tethered next to his goat.

"You sits very ooell on that horse," Head Sir compliments, improvising on the "turban" sentence. "Very ooell."

The Minister laughs, pleased. "One day there ooill be a motor road to this village, and I ooill arrive in a jeep!"

The village tour begins, the Minister followed by an entourage of local leaders and young children. Head Sir works his way to the front of the pack and points out the sites, in English.

"This is the pond, the Forestry Office, the shop . . ."

"My shop," Lal shouts from behind. "Come inside."

Lal leads the Minister into the shop, a dark and dusty room lined with shelves. There are faded posters on the walls, advertisements of products, mostly Indian. There is an ad for soap, a beautiful Indian woman lovingly holding a bar. The ad for baby formula depicts the god Krishna as a fat and laughing baby with blue skin. The shelves hold matches and razor blades, soap and ballpoint pens. On the floor, onions, potatoes, and rock salt are piled on dusty burlap sacking. Lal has a hand scale to weigh out kilos of goods. Rice and lentils are sold by volume from burlap sacks, a *maana* measured out in a small brass cup.

"Of course, it is not as fine as the shops in Kathmandu," he apologizes, offering the Minister a cigarette.

"It is a very fine shop," the Minister protests.

"Ah, yes," Head Sir muses in English. "The grace of angels. He who has the grace of the angels acquires the ooisdom of the gods. Is that not so, Minister?"

The Minister bows his head. "Your English is very good, my friend. But I fear the others cannot understand us."

"He who ooould ooalk with the gods must speak their language."

The Minister laughs.

The entourage has waited patiently through this exchange of English. But the Mayor grows restless. "Come look at our forestry project on the hill, Minister," he says in Nepali. "Our village is fighting the battle against deforestation and erosion. And we are winning!" And the group shuffles up the hill. Shastri says a prayer over the rows of saplings. The Mayor thanks him. The Minister proposes that if every village would take care of its surrounding land, erosion could be halted in its tracks.

"He who ooould climb to the stars must first secure his ladder," Head Sir agrees solemnly. He and the Mayor jostle each other, vying for position to help the Minister down the hill. At one point the men have each grabbed one of the Minister's arms.

The Mayor has hired several local musicians to play in the evening as the food is prepared. The band includes a flute and a pair of cymbals, keeping time with a two-toned drum. A large fire is built near the tent.

The Mayor leads the goat past the tent for the Minister's approval. Shastri prepares the goat for sacrifice. He rinses the goat's hind quarters. He asks the goat's permission to be sacrificed, tossing water in its ears. The goat stands still, stubbornly. Shastri asks again, tossing more water, and the goat assents, shaking its head. Shastri says a short prayer as the goat's neck is stretched taut, the Mayor pulling the rope at the front, a young boy holding the goat's hind legs. The teashop proprietor raises a large *kukri* over his head, its curved blade finely sharpened for the sacrifice. Shastri closes his eyes. The goat chokes and coughs as the rope pulls against its neck. But the sacrifice is auspicious, the proprietor clearing the neck in one stroke. Shastri opens his eyes in time to see the goat's head blink once in surprise.

A bucket is placed under the goat's neck to catch the blood; blood pudding will be made. The body is then singed on the fire, filling the campsite with the smell of burned hair. The stomach is removed and cleaned, then filled with beaten eggs to bake like custard. The teashop proprietor's two daughters sit under a tree making leaf plates and talking. A huge pot of rice is prepared, the vegetables are cooked. The proprietor hacks the goat into small pieces. Meat, bone and gristle will all be cooked and served together, leaving the real work to the diners.

Head Sir is delighted to find that the Minister is a drinker. The Mayor, Lal and Head Sir sit under the tent, plying flattery and *raksi* on the Minister. Shastri sits with them, beaming. Head Sir seems to get on quite well with the Minister. The men drink heavily. At seven, Shastri goes home to eat with his family. When he returns at nine, he finds that the men are just starting to eat. The teashop proprietor's daughters serve the men, ladling out meat and vegetables. The men eat with their hands. Head Sir is quite drunk and a few grains of rice stick to the stubble on his cheeks. *Raksi* is called for and when the supply is gone, a runner is sent to the Mayor's house for more.

"So, friend, what do you think of our village?" the Mayor asks the Minister.

"Very nice," the Minister responds, looking at the full hips of the two girls.

Head Sir follows the Minister's glance and chuckles conspiratorially. "The beauty of heaven is found on earth in a beautiful oooman," Head Sir comments. "Truth is beauty, beauty truth, eh, brother?"

"True," the Minister replies. The girls become shy. Instinctively they tuck their *saris* more securely over their breasts, and look at the ground. "You must all come visit me when you come to Kathmandu," the Minister says, expansively. He takes a little more *raksi*.

The moment has come and Head Sir plunges in. "I wanted to ask, brother, if the services of a man like me could be used in your office?"

Shastri gasps. The other men stop eating.

Head Sir falters, then adds, "A brave man is a ooarrior for any just cause."

The Minister scrutinizes Head Sir, nodding slowly. "Perhaps. I will survey the situation when I return to my office."

"I can meet you in Kathmandu when you return."

"Wait a little while, friend," the Minister says. "I will send a telegram when the time is right."

Head Sir is elated. He avoids Shastri's glance.

"You is leaving here?" Shastri asks.

But Head Sir does not answer Shastri. "More *raksi* for the Minister!" he cries out. He sends one of the girls out for *raksi*. They both get up to leave together, but Head Sir forbids it. "You stay," he orders the prettier one. She watches her sister depart. "Come here," Head Sir says. The girl stands uncertainly at the edge of the tent. "Come here, beauty," he says again, clumsily patting the seat beside him. "Come sit by the Minister and me."

The girl hesitates. "Come here," Head Sir says. He pats his lap. "Here is a comfortable seat for those beautiful round hips." But the girl flees the tent, and Head Sir and the Minister are laughing when her father arrives.

"You bastards," the proprietor says.

Lal and the Mayor stand up uncomfortably. They follow the proprietor out of the tent, trying to appease him. Shastri also stands. "You is drinking *raksi* there. Too much!" he says sternly. "You is too much *raksi* there." He marches out of the tent on his fat little legs. Head Sir and the Minister burst out laughing again.

Head Sir stumbles home to his *deraa* in the dark. It is very late and Head Sir expects to find Shastri there, as he usually does on a late night. But the *deraa* is empty. Head Sir lays down; the bed floats on *raksi*. He sleeps fitfully and awakens early, his head pounding and his throat dry.

Tea is brought to the Minister from down the road; the proprietor refuses to make it. Lal and the Mayor stand awkwardly by the Minister's tent. They mutter hasty farewells and flee. Word is spreading in the village about the previous night's insult; the men wish to distance themselves from the scene.

Head Sir goes to the water tap to douse his throbbing head. Shastri is there, performing his morning prayers. Head Sir interrupts him. "Eh, Shastri *ji*. Did you sleep well?"

"I'm praying," Shastri snaps. "Go ask the Minister how *he* slept."

Head Sir is taken aback. He opens his mouth, then shuts it. Shastri's eyes are closed in prayer. Head Sir rinses under the cold water and hurries to the Minister's tent.

The Minister is preparing to leave. He sees Head Sir and nods.

"Good morning, brother," Head Sir says. "Did you sleep ooell?"

"So-so," the Minister answers. "I must be off. I have a meeting in the District Center this afternoon." The Minister is helped onto his horse.

"Very ooell." Head Sir strokes the horse's flank. "I'll be ooaiting for that telegram."

"Telegram? Ah, yes," the Minister nods solemnly. "Good things come to those who ooait, but patience has its own reooards."

"On ooings of eagles I ooill fly to your side."

Head Sir watches the Minister ride away. The porters are packing up the tent, loading the equipment into baskets, the camp site growing strangely empty. The large firepit is a charred patch of ground, dark stains mark the goat's demise. The Minister's possessions are portered out of sight and Head Sir is left to weigh his gains, and losses.

Barbara Kerley

Barbara Kerley served as a math and science teacher with the Peace Corps in Nepal from 1981-83. There she met her future husband, Scott Kelly, also a Peace Corps Volunteer. During that time she was able to travel to India and the interior of Nepal, the inspiration for her story, "The Brave Ooarrior".

Born in Washington, DC, Kerley received a BA in English literature from the University of Chicago, and an MA in English literature and a MATESL (Master of Arts Teaching English as a Second Language) from the University of Washington where she won a National Resource Foundation fellowship to study Hindi in 1986.

Her stories have appeared in the *Clinton Street Quarterly* and *The Arts*, the King County arts newsletter.

In 1990 she returned to the United States after two years in Micronesia where she had been teaching English as a second language at the University of Guam.

Kerley currently lives in northern California with her husband and baby, Anna. She has completed a series of stories set in Nepal and, "When motherhood permits," is at work on a novel set in Micronesia.

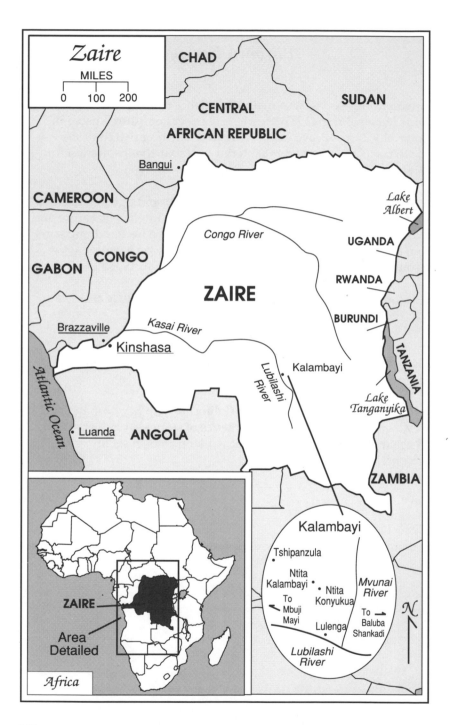

Zaire

MILES
0   100   200

CHAD

SUDAN

CENTRAL

AFRICAN REPUBLIC

Bangui .

CAMEROON

Lake
Albert

Congo River

UGANDA

GABON   CONGO

RWANDA

ZAIRE

BURUNDI

Brazzaville

Kasai River

• Kinshasa

Lubilashi
River

Kalambayi

TANZANIA

Lake
Tanganyika

Atlantic Ocean

• Luanda   ANGOLA

ZAMBIA

ZAIRE

Area
Detailed

Africa

Kalambayi

• Tshipanzula

Ntita
Kalambayi • • Ntita
Konyukua

Mvunai
River

To
Mbuji
Mayi

To
Baluba
Shankadi

Lulenga

N

Lubilashi
River

ILUNGA'S HARVEST

Mike Tidwell

"**M**y wife has left me, and I've got to harvest my pond," Chief Ilunga said. It was two o'clock on a Sunday afternoon and he was breathing hard. He had just walked the five miles from his village of Ntita Kalambayi to my house in Lulenga. He had walked quickly, stopping only once to drink *tshitshampa* with friends along the way. Now his speech was excited, full of the fast cadence of personal crisis. "My wife has left me, and I've got to harvest my pond. I've got to harvest it tomorrow and use the money to get her back."

It was a dowry dispute. Ilunga's father-in-law claimed Ilunga still owed thirty dollars in bridewealth from the marriage to his daughter five years earlier. To emphasize the point, he had ordered his daughter home to their village thirty miles away. She had obeyed, taking with her all the children. Now Ilunga was humiliated and alone, with no one to cook his food or wash his clothes. He needed money fast.

The development was something of a blow to me, too. Never had I expected the first fruits of my extension work to go toward something as inglorious as roping in a runaway wife. But that's what the Fates had snipped off. I told Ilunga I would be at his pond the next morning to help with the harvest.

Ilunga's wife had picked a bad time to leave him. His pond was in its fifth month of production, one month short of the

141

gestation period best for harvesting. Still, after only five months, things looked good. Ilunga had fed his fish like a man possessed, and as far as we could tell a considerable bounty waited below.

Part of the pond's success was due to a strategy I had developed not long after arriving in Kalambayi. The plan was simple: get Ilunga and the other farmers to feed their fish with the same intensity they fed me *fufu*, and they would surely raise some of the biggest tilapia ever recorded.

"Imagine a fish is like an important visitor who has traveled over mountains and through rivers to see you," I had told Ilunga after he finished his pond. "If, when you set a meal down in front of that visitor, he finishes all the food in two or three minutes and then stares back at you from across the table, how do you feel?"

He grimaced. "Terrible," he said. "The visitor is still hungry. He should always be given more food than he can eat. He shouldn't be able to finish it. That's how you know he's full."

"Exactly," I said.

Exactly. Every day for five months, Ilunga dumped more food into his pond than his fish could possible eat. He covered the surface with sweet potato leaves and manioc leaves and papaya leaves, and the fish poked and chewed and started to grow.

Helping things out was an unexpected gift. Two months after we stocked the pond, an official of the United Nations Children's Fund in Mbuji Mayi donated two sturdy wheelbarrows to the Kalambayi fish project. The wheelbarrows were blue with "UNICEF" painted neatly on the sides in white. When I called all the farmers together to present the tools, the shiny steel basins and rubber tires inspired a great amount of whistling and head-shaking. I felt as if I had just delivered two mint-condition Mack trucks. The men ran their hands along the rims and grew dizzy contemplating the wealth the tools might bring. Using the village of Kabala as a dividing point, the farmers split up into two committees representing the upper and lower stretches of the Lubilashi River. After establishing rules for their use, the men took possession of the wheelbarrows.

Ilunga, as much as anyone, parlayed the UNICEF largess into bigger fish. He used the upper Kalambayi wheelbarrow to gather leaves and termites for fish food. To fill his pond's stick compost bins he went most Thursdays to the weekly outdoor market in Ntita Konyukua. There, he used the wheelbarrow to collect manioc peels and fruit rinds and the other rubbish village markets leave scattered about the ground. These materials rot quickly in pond water, stimulating a plankton growth essential for intensive tilapia culture. But to get the goods, Ilunga had to swallow his pride. He had to hunt through the crowd of marketeers and bend over and compete with hungry dogs and goats and chickens along the ground. It was something of a spectacle. Ilunga was thirty years old and the chief of a village—and he was shooing away goats to get at banana peels in the marketplace dirt. People started to talk. After a while, one of Ilunga's brothers tried to dissuade him of the practice. "You're embarrassing yourself," he said. "The pond isn't worth this."

But Ilunga didn't listen, just as he hadn't listened back in the beginning when I told him he was digging a pond so large it might kill him. He kept going to the market. Stares and whispers didn't stop him.

Most amazing was the fact that Ilunga was doing all this work in addition to tending his fields every day like everyone else. He was squeezing two jobs from the daily fuel of protein-deficient *fufu*. Eventually it started to show. I walked to his house one afternoon and found him outside, fast asleep in the coddling embrace of the UNICEF wheelbarrow. He had lined the basin with a burlap sack and reposed himself, his arms and legs drooping over the edges. From the trail fifty feet away, I watched. The imagery was potent, almost unbearable with its themes of hope and struggle and want all bound up in that exhausted face, those closed eyes, those dirty black limbs hanging down to the ground. God, how I had set Ilunga's soul ablaze with my talk of rising out of poverty, of beating back the worst aspects of village life with a few fish ponds. He had listened to me and followed every line of advice and now he lay knocked out in the hold of a donated wheelbarrow. Deciding it would be criminal to wake him, I walked away, praying like hell that all the promises I had made were true.

And now we would find out. It was time for the denoue-ment: the harvest. Five months had passed, Ilunga's wife had left him and we would discover what had been happening all this time under the pond's surface. I was anxious because, in a way, owning a fish pond is like owning a lottery ticket. Unlike corn, which you can watch as it grows, or, say, chickens, which you can weigh as they get big, there is no way to positively assess the progress of a pond until you harvest it. The fish are under the water, so you can't count them or get a good look at them. You just have to work and work and wait. You hang on to your lottery ticket and wait for the drawing, never sure what number will come up until you drain the pond.

Ilunga and I had a pretty good idea his fish were big, of course. God knows they had been given enough to eat. We also had seen lots of offspring along the pond's edges. But the water was now so well fertilized and pea-green with plankton that neither of us had seen a fish in nearly two months. (Ilunga had refused to eat any fish in order to maximize the harvest.) We knew the tilapia were there, but how many exactly? How big? And what about the birds? How many fish had the thieving kingfishers taken? We would soon know all the answers. An unacknowledged, icy fear ran through both of us as we agreed that Sunday afternoon at my house to harvest his pond the next day.

It was just past 6 am when I arrived for the harvest. Ilunga and his brother Tshibamba were calling and waving their arms as I moved down the valley slope toward the pond. "Michel, Michel. Come quickly. Hurry, Michel." I had driven my motorcycle to Ilunga's house in the predawn dark, using my headlight along the way. Now, as I finished the last of the twenty-minute walk to the valley floor, the sky was breaking blue and a crazy montage of pink and silver clouds lay woven on the horizon. The morning beauty was shattered, however, by the cries of the men waiting for me at the pond. They were yelling something I didn't want to hear. It was something my mind refused to accept.

"There are no fish, Michel," they said. "Hurry. The fish aren't here."

I reached the pond and cast an incredulous stare into the water. They were right. There were no fish. The men had spent most of the night digging out a vertical section of the lower dike and slowly draining the water until there now remained only a muddy, five-by-five-foot pool in the lower-most corner of the pond. The pool was about six inches deep. And it was empty.

Tshibamba was screaming, running along the dikes and pointing an accusing finger at the pond bottom. "Where are the fish?"

Ilunga was past the yelling stage. He gazed at the shallow pool, his face sleepy and creased, and said nothing. He was a wreck; as forlorn and defeated as the pond scarecrow ten feet to his left with its straw limbs akimbo and head splotched with bird excrement.

"Wait a minute," I said to the men, suddenly spotting something at one end of the pool. "Look!"

I pointed to a fan-shaped object sticking out of the water and looking a lot like a dorsal fin. We all looked. It moved. A fish. Before we could celebrate, other fins appeared throughout the pool, dozens of them, then hundreds. The pond water, which had continued all the while to flow out through a net placed over the cut dike, had suddenly reached a depth lower than the vertical height of the bottom-hugging fish. The fish had been hiding under the muddy water and were revealed only at the last moment and all at the same time, a phenomenon of harvesting we eventually became nervously accustomed to in Kalambayi. Ilunga's fish—big, medium and small—had been corralled by the dropping water into the small pool where they waited like scaly cattle. They looked stupid and restless. "Yeah, now what?" they seemed to ask.

Ilunga showed them. He threw off his shirt and made a quick banzai charge into the congested fray, his arms set to scoop up hard-won booty. There ensued an explosion of jumping fish and flying mud, and Ilunga absorbed the rat-tat-tat of a thousand mud dots from his feet to his face. By the time his hands reached the pool, the fish had scattered everywhere into the surrounding mud like thinking atoms suddenly released from some central, binding force. Ilunga raised his empty hands. He looked up at us—his face covered with mud dots, his feet sinking into the pond-bottom gook—and flashed a wide smile. The harvest had begun.

"The small ones," I yelled, hurriedly discarding my shirt and shoes. "Get the small fish first to restock with."

I jumped into the pond and, like Ilunga, was immediately pelted with mud. Two more of Ilunga's brothers had arrived by then, and together, five strong, we gave battle with the tenacity of warriors waging *jihad*. We chased the flapping, flopping, fleeing fish through the pond-bottom sludge. When we caught them, we stepped on them and throttled them and herded them into tin buckets. Ilunga took charge of capturing and counting three hundred thumb-sized stocking fish and putting them in a small holding pond. The rest of us collected the other fish, segregating the original stockers, which were now hand-sized, from the multitudinous offspring. The work was dirty and sloppy and hypnotically fun.

So engrossed was I in the harvest, in fact, that I barely noticed the tops of the pond dikes were growing crowded with onlookers. By the time we finished capturing all the fish, people had surrounded the square pond bottom like spectators around a boxing ring. A quarter of the men, women, and children in the village had come to see the harvest. I was impressed by their show of support for Ilunga's work.

Ilunga ordered the crowd to clear back from a spot on the upper dike. Filthy like pigs, we carried the fish out of the pond in four large buckets and set them down at the clearing. We rinsed them off with canal water and began weighing them with a small hand-held scale I had brought. The total came to forty-four kilos. It was an excellent harvest. After only five months, Ilunga had coaxed three hundred tilapia fingerlings into forty-four kilos of valuable protein. It was enough to bring home his wife and then some.

Whistling and laughing, I grabbed Ilunga by the shoulders and shook him and told him what a great harvest it was. I had expected a lot of fish, but not this many. It was marvelous, I told him, simply marvelous. He smiled and agreed. But he wasn't nearly as happy as he should have been. Something was wrong. His eyes telegraphed fear.

Tshibamba made the first move.

"Go get some leaves from that banana tree over there," he told a child standing on the pond bank.

When the child returned, Tshibamba scooped about a dozen fish onto one of the leaves and wrapped them up.

"I'm going to take these up to the house," he said to Ilunga. "It's been a while since the children have had fresh fish."

"Yes, yes," Ilunga said. "Take some."

"I'll have a little, too," said Kazadi, Ilunga's youngest brother, reaching into a bucket.

"Go ahead. Take what you need."

Then a third brother stepped forward. Then a fourth. Then other villagers. My stomach sank.

It was suddenly all clear—the crowd, the well-wishers, the brothers of Ilunga who had never even seen the pond until that morning. They had come to divide up the harvest. A cultural imperative was playing itself out. It was time for Ilunga to share his wealth. He stood by the buckets and started placing fish in the hands of every relative and friend who stepped forth. He was just giving the harvest away.

There was no trace of anger on his face as he did it, either. Nor was there a suggestion of duty or obligation. It was less precise than that. This was Ilunga's village and he had a sudden surplus and so he shared it. It just happened. It was automatic. But the disappointment was there, weighing down on the corners of his eyes. He needed the fish. Getting his wife back had depended on them.

Caked in mud, I sat on the grassy bank and watched an entire bucket of tilapia disappear. Fury and frustration crashed through me with the force of a booming waterfall. All that work. All my visits. All the digging and battling kingfishers. All for what? For this? For a twenty-minute free-for-all give-away? Didn't these people realize the ponds were different? Ilunga had worked hard to produce this harvest. He had tried to get ahead. Where were they when he dug his pond? Where were they when he heaved and hoed and dislodged from the earth 4,000 cubic feet of dirt?

I knew the answer. They had been laughing. They had been whispering among themselves that Ilunga was wasting his time, that moving so much dirt with a shovel was pure lunacy. And they laughed even harder when they saw him bending over to pick up fruit rinds in the marketplace in competition with goats and dogs. But they weren't laughing now. Ilunga had proved them wrong. He had raised more fish than any of them had seen in their lives, and now they were taking the spoils.

The fish continued to disappear and I began bursting with a desire to intervene. I wanted to ask Ilunga what the hell he was doing and to tell him to stop it. I wanted to turn over the bucket already emptied of fish and stand on it and shoo everyone away like I had shooed Mutoba Muenyi those first few times she came to my door. "Giving is virtuous and all that," I wanted to tell the crowd. "But this is different. These are Ilunga's fish. They're *his*. Leave them alone. He needs them."

But I said nothing. I summoned every ounce of self-restraint in my body and remained silent. This was something between Ilunga and his village. My job was to teach him how to raise fish. I had done my job. What he did with the fish afterward really was none of my business. Even so, I didn't have to watch. I went over to the canal and washed up. Ilunga was well into the second bucket when I told him I was leaving.

"Wait," he said. "Here."

He thrust into my hands a large bundle of fish.

Oh, no, I thought. Not me. I'm not going to be party to this gouging. I tried to hand the bundle back.

"But these fish are for you," he said. "You've taught me how to raise fish, and this is to say thank you."

"No, Ilunga. This is your harvest. You earned it. You keep it."

He gave me a wounded look, as if I had just spit in his face, and suddenly I wanted to scream and kick and smash things. I couldn't refuse his offer without devastating him. I took the fish and headed up the hill, feeling like a real parasite.

"Wait for me at the house," he said as I walked away.

It was 8:30 when I reached the village and stretched out, dizzy with disappointment, on a reed mat next to Ilunga's house. He arrived about thirty minutes later with his sister Ngala who had helped at the harvest. Both of their faces looked drained from the great hemorrhaging they had just gone through. Without even the benefit of loaves of bread, they had fed a mass of about fifty villagers, and now Ngala carried all that was left in one big tin basin. I estimated there were about twenty-five kilos. To my dismay, though, Ilunga wasn't finished. He scooped out another couple of kilos to give to older relatives who hadn't made it to the pond. Then he sent Ngala off to the market in Lulenga with roughly twenty-three kilos of fish, barely half the harvest total.

At the going market price of 100 zaires a kilo, Ilunga stood to make 2300 zaires ($23). It was far short of what he needed to get his wife back. Far short, in fact, of anything I could expect village men to accept as fair return for months of punishing shovel work and more months of maniacal feeding. The problem wasn't the technology. Ilunga had produced forty-four kilos of fish in one pond in five months. That was outstanding. The problem, rather, was generosity. It was a habit of sharing so entrenched in the culture that it made me look to the project's future with foreboding. What incentive did men like Ilunga have to improve their lives—through fish culture or any other means—if so much of the gain immediately melted into a hundred empty hands? Why work harder? Why develop? Better just to farm enough to eat. Better to stay poor like all the rest.

After Ilunga's sister left for the market, I couldn't hold my tongue any longer. We were alone at his house.

"I can't believe you gave away all those fish, Ilunga. Why did you even bother digging a pond if all you were going to do with the harvest was give it away?"

He knew I was upset, and he didn't want to talk about it.

"Why did you dig a pond?" I repeated.

"You know why," he said. "To get more money. To help my family."

"So how can you help your family if you give away half the

fish?"

"But there's still a lot left," he said. "You act like I gave them all away."

I suddenly realized he was about ten times less upset by what had happened than I was. My frustration doubled.

"What do you mean there's still a lot left? There's not enough to get your wife back, is there? You gave away too much for that. Your pond hasn't done you much good, and I guess I've wasted my time working with you."

The last sentence really annoyed him.

"Look," he said, "what could I have done? After I drained my pond I had hundreds and hundreds of fish. There were four buckets full. You saw them. If my brother comes and asks for ten fish, can I say no? For ten fish? That's crazy. I can't refuse."

"No, it's not crazy, Ilunga. You have six brothers and ten uncles and fifty cousins. And then there are all the other villagers. You're right. Ten fish aren't very many. But when you give ten to everyone you have little left for yourself."

"So what would you have done?" he asked me. "Would you have refused fish to all those people?"

"Yes," I said, and I meant it.

"You mean you would have taken all the fish and walked past all those people and children and gone up to the house and locked the door."

"Don't say it like that," I said. "You could have explained to them that the pond was your way of making money, that the harvest was for your wife."

"They already know I need my wife," he said. "And they know I'll get her back somehow."

"Yeah, how? You were counting on the harvest to do that, and now it's over. You gave away too much, Ilunga. You can't keep doing this. You can't feed the whole village by yourself. It's impossible. You have to feed your own children and take care of your own immediate family. Let your brothers worry about their families. Let them dig ponds if they want to. You've got to stop giving away your harvests."

Thus spoke Michel, the agent of change, the man whose job it was to try to rewrite the society's molecular code. Sharing *fufu* and produce and other possessions was one thing. With time, I had come around to the habit myself, seen its virtuosity. But the ponds were different, and I had assumed the farmers realized that. Raising fish was meant to create surplus wealth; to carry the farmers and their immediate families to a level where they had more for themselves—better clothes, extra income. That was the incentive upon which the project was built. It was the whole reason I was there.

So when Ilunga harvested his pond that early morning and started giving away the fish, I wanted to retreat. I wanted to renounce my conversion to the local system and move back to the old impulse I had arrived with, the one that had me eating secret, solitary meals and guarding my things in the self-interested way prized by my society.

"Stop the giving"—that was the real, the final, message I wanted to bring to Ilunga and the other fish farmers. Stop the giving and the community-oriented attitude and you can escape the worst ravages of poverty. Build a pond and make it yours. And when you harvest it, don't give away the fish. Forget, for now, the bigger society. Forget the extended family. Step back and start thinking like self-enriching entrepreneurs, like good little capitalists.

But Ilunga didn't fit the plan. Nor did any of the other farmers who harvested after him. "If my brother comes and asks for ten fish, can I say no?" he had asked. His logic was stronger than it seemed. Like everyone else in Kalambayi, Ilunga needed badly the help fish culture could provide. What he didn't need, however, were lessons on how to stay alive. And that, I eventually grew to understand, was what all the sharing was really about. It was a survival strategy; an unwritten agreement by the group that no one would be allowed to fall off the societal boat no matter how low provisions ran on board. No matter how bad the roads became or how much the national economy constricted, sharing and mutual aide meant everyone in each village stayed afloat. If a beggar like Mutoba Muenyi came to your house in the predawn darkness, you gave her food. If you harvested a pond and fifty malnourished relatives showed up, you shared what you had. Then you made the most of what was left. If it was twenty-three dollars, that was okay. It was still a lot of money in a country where the average annual income is $170 and falling. It might not pay off a marriage debt, but $23 satisfied other basic needs.

In the end, despite my fears, sharing didn't destroy the fish project. Farmers went on building and harvesting ponds, giving away twenty to fifty percent of their fish, and selling the rest to earn money for their wives and their children. It was a process I simply couldn't change and eventually I stopped trying.

And perhaps it was just as well Ilunga and the others weren't in a hurry to become the kind of producers I wanted them to be. They might develop along Western lines with time, but why push them? The local system worked. Everyone *was* taken care of. Everyone *did* stay afloat. Besides, there were already plenty of myopic, self-enriching producers in the world— entrepreneurs and businesses guided by the sole principle of increasing their own wealth above all else. So many were there in fact that the planetary boat, battered by breakneck production and consumption, was in ever-increasing danger of sinking, taking with it the ultimate extended family: the species. There seemed to be no survival strategy at work for the planet as a whole as there was for this small patch of Africa; no thread of broader community interest that ensured against total collapse. Indeed, sitting in my lamplit cotton warehouse at night, listening to growing reports of global environmental degradation over my shortwave radio, the thought occurred to me more than once that, in several important respects, Kalambayi needed far less instruction from the West than the other way around.

At the moment, however, no one needed anything as much as Ilunga needed his wife. He had given away nearly half his fish and now the opportunity had all but vanished. I stopped back by his house after the market closed in Lulenga and watched him count the money from the harvest: two thousand zaires. Even less than I thought. I reached into my pocket and pulled out all I had, two hundred zaires. I handed it to him. He was still short.

"What are you going to do?"

"I don't know," he said, "I've got to think about it."

Three days later, on my way to Tshipanzula, I pulled up to Ilunga's house to see what solution he had come up with. I was surprised when he wasn't there and his neighbors said he had gone to Baluba Shankadi, his wife's tribe.

Another week went by before I saw Ilunga again. It was in the market in Ntita Konyukua and he was standing under a mimosa tree, gesturing and talking with two other fish farmers. As I made my way through the crowd of marketeers, getting closer, I saw Ilunga's wife standing behind him, carrying their youngest child.

"How?" I asked when I reached him, shaking his hand, delighted by the sight of mother and child. "How did you do it?"

At first he didn't answer. He talked instead about his pond, telling me he had returned the day before and now was trying to track down the UNICEF wheelbarrow to start feeding his fish again.

"But your wife," I said. "How did you get her back?"

"Oh, yes, she's back," he said. "Well, I really don't know how I did it. After you left my house that day I still needed eight hundred zaires. One of my brothers gave me a hundred, but it still wasn't enough. I tried, but I couldn't come up with the rest of the money so I decided to leave with what I had. I walked for two days and reached my wife's village and handed the money to my father-in-law. He counted it and told me I was short. I told him I knew I was but that I didn't have any more. Then I knew there was going to be a big argument."

"Was there?"

"No. That's the really strange part. He told me to sit down, and his wife brought out some *fufu* and we ate. Then it got dark and we went inside to sleep. I still hadn't seen my wife. The next morning my father-in-law called me outside. Then he called my wife and my sons from another house. We were all standing in the middle of the compound, wondering what to do. Then he just told us to leave. 'That's it?' I said. 'It's over?' He told me yes, that I could go home. I didn't think I understood him correctly, so I asked him if he was sure he didn't want any more money. 'No, you've done enough,' he said. 'Go back to your village.' I was afraid to say anything else. I put my wife and my sons in front of me and we started walking away before he could change his mind."

Mike Tidwell

Mike Tidwell is descended from a long line of dirt farmers in central Tennessee and northern Mississippi. By the 1940s, the Great Depression had pushed part of the clan to Memphis where Tidwell's parents and, later, his sister were born in poverty and public housing. The family had begun to edge out of these circumstances only slightly by the time Tidwell was born in 1962. At the age of ten, he contributed to the running of a paper route that helped put his father through college.

With his family securely grounded in the middle class, Tidwell joined the Peace Corps in 1985. His experience as a fish culture extension agent in Zaire is told in *The Ponds of Kalambayi* (1990 Lyons and Burford, Publishers), from which "Ilunga's Harvest" is excerpted.

Tidwell graduated *magna cum laude* with a BA in political science from the University of Georgia where he also earned admission to Phi Beta Kappa. He now works as a drug counselor in Washington, DC, where he is a member of Servas, an international peace organization.

His writing has appeared in *The Progressive*, *The Christian Science Monitor*, *Sierra*, and *In These Times*. He is a former stringer and intern reporter for the *Atlanta Journal-Constitution* newspaper.

Tidwell is currently completing a non-fiction book about "skid row, crack addiction and class warfare" in the nation's capitol. Entitled *In the Shadow of the White House*, it is to be published by Prima Publishing in the fall of 1991.

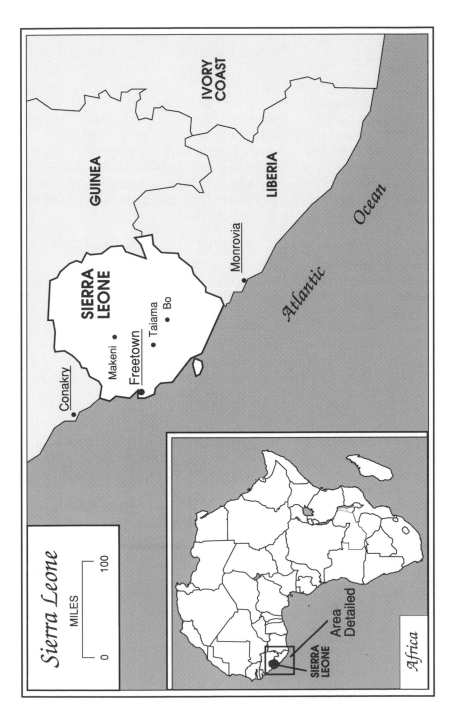

Sierra Leone

MILES

0   100

GUINEA

IVORY
COAST

LIBERIA

Monrovia

SIERRA
LEONE

Makeni

Freetown

Taiama

Bo

Conakry

Atlantic

Ocean

Area
Detailed

SIERRA
LEONE

Africa

MI PADI DOHN LEHF MI

Kinney Thiele

Scarecrows have dotted the Bo rice swamp now for weeks. At dawn they come to perch on bushstick platforms and sing up the day with greetings amongst their neighbors. Little human scarecrows they are, children who do not go to school, and others on holiday, sent by their families and chiefs to share a vital task.

As a flock of black and yellow weaver birds attacks, a swell of sound rushes with it, a surge and ebb past the veranda where I sit. Each boy joins the chorus at his post. With voice, gestures, sticks and clods, claps, drumming, and shouts, he hurls distractions at the sky from his arsenal of style and whims, then settles back to wait again.

It was cooler than usual this morning and I awoke late. At 7:00 a.m. I actually got 13 minutes of Voice of America and BBC news. It's old news: there's unrest in the Middle East; the Irish are bombing themselves; South Africans hurt each other and their mutual future. All claim God and right on their side.

Willy came to tell me the real news, the local news, all that really counts in the small world of the village: the old tailor is dead.

When I first moved to Taiama—a stranger—six weeks ago,

157

I wanted to make friends. Everyday as I walked over the rise behind our house and down toward the river to shop, I stopped to talk with Mr. Momoh at his house across from the mosque. Although Mende is his daily tongue, he began unwrapping English from the attic of his past, seeming to bring out new words each day. He became my friend.

The old man sewed patches on an antique treadle machine on his veranda and pounded the drum at the mosque five times each day to announce the times for prayers. The view from his seat encompassed the market pavilion, three buildings away, and the court *barre*, where justice, bureaucracy, dance, and school programs are performed.

Mr. Momoh's veranda also seems to be a gathering place for the disabled. A bright-eyed, dwarfed, hunch-backed man rests there or on the cool porch of the mosque. A lanky, healthier looking man sits with one leg up on the low wall and stares at me, but does not acknowledge my greetings. And a white-haired woman is often about, looking aimless, at sea in a society where women are always busy and silver hair is disguised with native dyes or discreetly covered by a head tie.

This is also the veranda were I buy *groundnuts*. A woman and a young man sit there to shuck and sell them. She keeps a bright cloth on her lap to catch the nuts. Chickens work over the discarded shells. Husking peanuts is hard on my hands and takes a lot of time. I prefer to pay the extra for their labor, even though I once thought it would be a productive way to save money while keeping time with visitors or passing dark evenings.

One day the old tailor said he would visit me on Sunday. And he did. Although I usually follow the recommended procedure and sit with most guests on the veranda, I invited him inside. We sat on hard, straight chairs at my little table, and sipped limeade with lots of sugar. He told me about his children, long grown and most now living far away in the capitol. He grumbled that they do not look after him in the ways of the past so he has had to adjust: he's learned to earn his food by sewing patches.

Mostly though he talked about God and the privilege he has

to pound the drum announcing prayers. Sometimes, he said, it is hard to get up for the first call at 4:30 in the morning but it is for God. A radiant smile crossed his face. He was proud of this responsibility.

On Saturday morning, two weeks ago, I visited him. I went up on the veranda with right hand outstretched. He bounded up, even bent with age. We both held our extended arms with our left hands—supporting the weight of friendship we felt in our greetings. His rheumy eyes wrinkled with smiles.

He promised to visit the next day. Could he see the photos again of my family and America? I'd like that, I assured him, but I was going to be in Bo that morning. I admired his clock. He confessed it belonged to another who let him keep it there to help mark time for the mosque. Again pride. God, he assured me, is great. "I have nothing to worry about, even in the hungry season. God always provides something in the end."

As the humid heat intensifies they shelter under palm-thatched roofs that dry and crackle to the slightest motion. When clouds and thunder threaten sudden rain, some scamper barefoot over dikes to find and pull free a giant banana leaf, an umbrella as fresh as each storm.

Some sneak nibbles under the berry trees hard by this house. Perhaps they believe they're invisible to me. If they notice that I see them, those in the open startle and run to escape imagined danger, while others freeze in shadows. Any I address directly are fatalistic, making no effort to escape. The brave ones tumble and swing high, seeking the tastier bites on fragile, bending tips of boughs, flirting with me as they stretch, tossing out grins and comments.

Willy says he saw Mr. Momoh yesterday on the veranda. He doesn't believe it yet. I believe. I know no details, but I hope he died in his sleep after the last prayers, and that when the time came for the predawn call, his friend, the bright-eyed dwarf, was there to pound awake all for prayers on our friend's first morning with his God.

It was late morning before Jonathan came to report, "They

are digging the hole now." Everything is hard to extract from Jonathan, partly because of language but largely because of our cultural differences. I daily find that assumptions of how to do things are meaningless—customs, expectations, style, habit, practice, behavior—these are socially taught in every culture, and subject to myriad variations and interpretations.

"When will they bury him?" I asked.

"After they dig the hole."

"Today?"

"Yes."

"Can I go?"

"Yes."

"Please tell me how I should do this."

"Go now."

"Are these clothes OK?" I asked, looking down at my cotton skirt and T-shirt.

"Yes."

I tucked a scarf into my pocket and we hiked off, up over the hill and down into town, wending our way through an unfamiliar maze of kitchen yards and paths to the house of the wake. I heard it from a distance, because of the sung prayers rising over the usual village hum.

Jonathan marched me straight up the veranda steps, and through a crowd of seated men to a chair vacated by a younger one for me. It appeared to be the correct courtesy for this event given my foreignness, at least in Jonathan's eyes. We shook hands all around and I accepted the seat. I felt uneasy. As a stranger, educated and white, I'm often treated as a "big man." This seems contrary to the Islamic custom of separating men and women, but the Mende are Africans first, and Islamic (or Christian) second.

People asked Jonathan some questions, then I said a few words about Mr. Momoh's kindness to me. Suddenly all curiosity and tension seemed to ease. They smiled in recognition. Something I said about him must have qualified me as having earned the right to mourn—a small edge above expected courtesies.

160

Mr. Carew, an elderly gentleman I shared broken-down transport with a few weeks back, looked steadily out from my right and gave the benediction: "When a person is alive and you love him, you love him when he dies."

I had already learned that it is the custom to give money to bereaved families. Everyone knows how much. Mr. Carew tells me it is insurance. I thought I understood his meaning, but he fortunately continued. "You see," he said, "we are all connected. We must pay our debts and end our quarrels when there is a death. You see, it is all written and remembered." In his hand was a school notebook with each detail noted.

We waited perhaps two hours on the veranda. Someone would come; another would go. A teacher arrived, a new face to me. He sat exactly opposite and began a long diatribe about the unfairness of life in this country. I said a lot of mmms. A university student chimed in and continued the familiar litany about abuse of power, nepotism, rechanneling of foreign aid. I listened to it all intently. I want to learn.

I've heard many speak from the perspective of the "in" side, those born to the correct family, voting for the correct candidates, in positions where they receive gifts for their help in gaining access to needs, or receiving allowances from government. These two seemed to be in the recently educated fringe between in and out, on their way toward Africanizing western thought and westernizing African thought. I'm afraid of politics. The most I will say in these situations is to repeat a few words, to underscore an especially good insight or plan they may suggest. I burn to have a lively discussion.

More people came on the veranda. The tall one-eyed man who welcomed me to town with two eggs was there. I noticed recently that when he is doing close-up work he wears a pair of glasses. The lens over the empty socket is fine, the one on the usable eye is shattered.

A stranger tested my Mende greeting skills, then began pressing important new Mende sentences on me.

"Be-kay-kay-bee-aye?"	(What's your father's name?)
"Bean njay bee-aye?"	(What's your mother's name?)
"Big bee-aw-mee doe?"	(Where do you come from?)

I was grateful to Mr. Carew who held him gently in check after three questions, explaining there are absorption limits.

After a time a lull in conversation gave me a period just to observe. The men all wore hats of some sort, from beanies to crocheted Islamic caps. One sported a western fedora. Another had on a ski cap with "Genesee" knitted across the front. I didn't get the feeling that anyone dressed for the occasion, except that the women wore prayer scarves.

The paunchy old woman arrived, the one who boldly moves about town uncovered from snowy crown to waist. I'd never heard her speak, but recognized her as part of the circle of somewhat disabled people who shared my friend's veranda. She came now wailing up the incline, hushed herself inside the house where prayers were being chanted responsively, but fled soon, to wail leaning against a tree, a wall, another wall, as she wandered, desolate. Another, young woman, came suddenly from inside and wept for a time. I'm told one may not cry in prayers.

Three long sticks, poles really, were brought. I thought they might be for carrying the coffin, but quickly saw the patina of long handling. Sure enough, the women began the 1-2-3 thud of pounding rice in one hardwood mortar. They say there is an art to pounding for each ingredient, and those of certain knowledge can recognize this rhythmical score for a recipe.

At noon the equatorial sun hides our shadows beneath our feet. Magic seems to still the birds, and the field empties for a few minutes. Chop time at home, a pot of rice and peppery green sauce floating in red palm oil is shared in fingersful beside the embers of three-stone fires.

They're quickly back and the day grows long. Between hungry swarms diving and striking at the nodding heads of rice, the scarecrows drowse. One recites Islamic prayers. Sisters wander out along the dikes with siblings on their hips, bringing calabashes of water or fresh palm fronds atop their heads as gifts.

Obviously, they were going to eat. I wanted to do the same. Mr. Carew got up, saying he would be back in awhile. As I feel best able to consult with him, I asked when the burial might be—an hour—and if it was correct that I go. He assured me that I should, and that if I wanted to leave for a time before then, that too would be fine. I don't entirely trust Jonathan's advice, as well-intentioned as it may be. He hasn't the wisdom to comprehend my ignorance. Mr. Carew knows to answer what I don't know to ask.

A quick trip to market, and home for a fresh canteen of water, and we went back. The coffin box was there, leaning up against the veranda wall. The body, wrapped in white cotton, was soon brought out on a flat pallet that I would have called the lid. After a pillow was placed under his head, the box was set atop. It took me a minute to get over feeling the coffin was upside-down. Then men lifted it all and carried it to the mosque yard. It was carefully laid with feet to the north, head south. The lid was removed, and the shroud opened around his eyes (though not revealing his face). The men lined up and facing east over his body, chanted prayers.

I stayed with the women this time, though I was invited to join the men. We stayed across the street around the place where he had sewn. They chattered while prayers were said. I was introduced to his widow, who appeared to get no other special treatment. I watched her. She seemed to huddle slightly against the wall, a bit downcast. When they covered the coffin finally, she strained up a little to see over our heads.

As we left the mosque to walk to the burial ground, the white-haired woman cried but stayed behind. It's about a mile, up from the river, over my hill, down across the rice swamp where people bathe and brook clothes, and up another slight hill through a wooded bush area. All of a sudden the women all stopped while the men continued up the hill and into the bush. After a time I heard chanting, then a young man trotted back carrying the top of the coffin.

Boredom in the fields generates a new wave of greetings. "Piskoh, piskoh," they call. I wave and greet and listen to their laughter. "Bobos" or "titis", boys or girls, approach my veranda, toting a "pekin", a smaller child. Some tiny ones are afraid of me, the stranger known as "poomwee," white one. Others fan their fingers and stretch to pat my hand. Soberly. Seriously. No smiles.

The women sat or stood, talking casually, stretching. In a flurry of playfulness one lifted another's blouse, pulled out a big wad of padding from one side of her bra, and teased her for being so under-endowed. A young woman who is utterly flat-chested, patted herself and shrugged. Other women felt themselves and each other through their clothes, showing off a sag here, an uplift there. I wasn't spared the inspection. (Even men have touched me casually as they ask if I have children.)

Time was passing. A woman found a feather, stripped it of all the fluff except half an inch at the tip, then whirled it in her ears. Another rocked the infant on her back in a gentle dancing step—left, close, right, close. I was, as usual, thirsty. I pulled out my flask and a cup, poured a drink and took it, then poured the remainder of the liter in small splashes for the other women. They accepted.

Mommy Hawa, leading the women, separated herself and walked about 200 feet to an opening in the bush that leads to the grave. She waved to the 40 or so of us to follow. They all bent down for pebbles. Mommy Hawa gave me one. I thought I saw many in her hand so I started to reach for more. A chorus of murmurs said no. I obeyed, but was curious. At the opening there was a bucket of water. Into it we each dropped a pebble. "Why?" I asked. I had expected to drop it in the grave, Christian-style. I learned later that the number of stones represents the number of people who've gone to the grave (about 150 on this day). The water is for the men to wash away death.

We women all left.

I asked if only women go to the grave of women. They told me but the answer was lost in our mismatch of languages. Few women speak Krio or English and my Mende is poor and unreliable. I think both men and women go, but they hastened to say women aren't needed at a grave; the men do the work. Also, they pointed out, it's an awfully long walk.

Shadows lengthen into the most beautiful light of the day. At a distant edge of the swamp, smoke pours through the thatch of a kitchen bafa. A farmer bathes nearby, naked in the swamp's feeder stream. Now the children are joined by men, many in business suits, trousers rolled up, shoes in one hand, an umbrella for shade or rain in the other. They finger the filling heads of rice and gaze out to the hills. The sun shimmers off the crop, sparkles; retreats from flooded ditches, drops away.

I left the homeward procession as we passed the path to my house at the edge of town. It had been a long day. I'd barely eaten all day. A houseful of guests waited to greet me and keep time. I wanted to rest. People kept talking. More came by. Finally, my only recourse was to leave.

I went to the clinic to check on the preparations for visitors Tuesday. As I was leaving there Fauzi, our Lebanese merchant, came by and began talking.

Mr. Momoh had worked for Fauzi's family more than 60 years. He never stole from them. Fauzi closed the store today in Mr. Momoh's honor.

Fauzi was shaken by the old white-haired woman's crying. "She cried and cried, she truly cried from her heart, although she is crazy," he said. "She was once the richest woman in town, clever in business. Then her mind slipped away, about ten years ago. Every morning Pa Momoh gave her food. She was his sister."

"She cried for him," Fauzi continued, "and she cried out for herself, 'Who will give me food?' She often wails, but today it was different. Today she understood. Today it was from the heart."

In the last fleeting instants of the tropical day, we, birds and people hasten to our shelters.

As I went on, alone, towards the sunset over the swollen river, I remembered the hunchbacked man. He'd come to me through the funeral crowd, looked up with faun eyes and said softly, *"Teeday me padi dohn die. Ee dohn lehf me."*

Kinney Thiele

Born in Ashland, Oregon, Kinney Thiele spent her childhood in several Oregon cities, establishing a life's pattern of change and movement. Her undergraduate education took place at six colleges across the country. She also has earned an MEd from the University of Massachusetts, Amherst.

Thiele raised her son, Rett, while employed as a secretary, seminar coordinator, and research analyst at SRI International in Menlo Park, California, where she has been since 1976. She is a member of the Northern California and National Council of Returned Peace Corps Volunteers, the American Red Cross, the American Association of Retired Persons, the California Academy of Sciences and the L.S.B. Leaky Foundation.

Interspersed with "many happy journeys" throughout the United States, Thiele has traveled extensively in Northern Europe, Kenya, the Soviet Union, Canada and New Zealand. She served as a health and rural development Volunteer with the Peace Corps in Sierra Leone in 1985-87. Her story, "Mi Padi Dohn Lehf Mi" derives from her experience in the Chiefdom of Kori.

An armchair Africanist since 1973, Thiele has mounted several exhibits of Sierra Leonean artifacts, paintings, and photographs in the San Francisco Bay area. She is a frequent lecturer on Africa and cross-cultural education at schools and colleges and has been a guest on a number of public affairs television programs.

Thiele is currently at work on a book about a "middle-aged woman's awe and fascination" in serving in the Peace Corps.

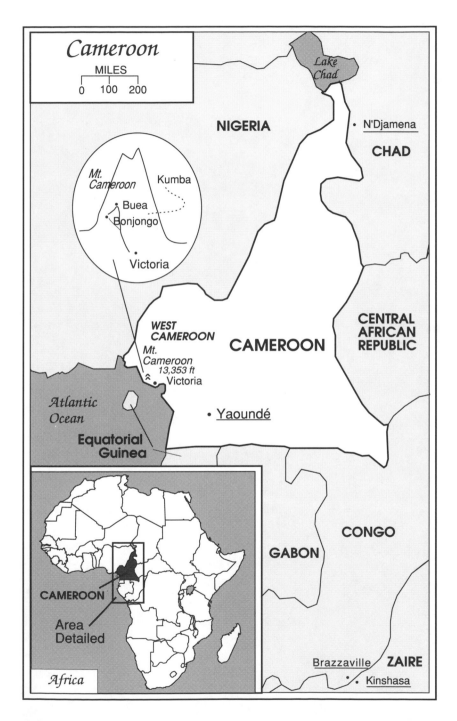

GARY AND THE PIGS

Mary-Ann Tirone Smith

Buea, pronounced, Boo-yuh, the toy-sized capital of West Cameroon, is made up of little whitewashed houses meandering about the side of Mt. Cameroon at five thousand feet. A winding road that begins in Buea makes its way down the mountainside to Victoria on the sea dividing the centuries-old Bakweri village from the modern town of two one-story government buildings and the houses of the officials and clerks who work in them. The benevolent convergence of lifestyles between Buea-village and Buea-town is reflected in the confluence of nature which takes place at this altitude. Towering alpine evergreens parade right out into the rain forest blanketing all of the mountain below Buea so that you find pine cones under ebony and mahogany trees. Except when the cooling rains come, the weather stays in the balmy seventies.

The first German colonial governor of Kamerun built his miniature schloss on a ledge above Buea—a baby castle looking down on a toy town. The Prime Minister lives in the schloss now, and what was once the German governor's botanical garden and rose bower is a prison farm, a smoothly-run dairy. The prisoners in their white coveralls and sanitary caps tend the cows and produce milk and cheese and butter to sell.

Once a week, I scooter up the steep incline to the prison with my friend Elizabeth Ebenego clinging to me from the back seat of my Honda. We buy milk for the children of the Buea Nursery School, and chat about the weather with the prisoners and guards.

"Good morning, Miss Elizabeth, Miss Maureen."

"Good morning."

"Let us hope the rains this year will be mild."

"Yes, let us hope."

The prisoners at the Buea prison farm weren't dangerous criminals. They were there because they refused to settle boundary disputes. Or they wouldn't go along with their tribe's dispersion of crops. The prison farm was a cooling-off spot for people with their noses out of joint. Tribes handled real crime through their secret societies.

I spent my days organizing a public library in Buea-village and helping out at Elizabeth's nursery school in Buea-town. I was grateful the Peace Corps stationed me in Buea. I loved the quaint village and the bustling town, and I loved the Bakweries and the mountain, and the sea below, and my friend Elizabeth, and the friendly prisoners, too. I loved my little two-room, cement block house and my half-civet cat, Boo, named after my home. Buea was home.

One evening the harmony and tranquility of my happy Buea home was jolted by the arrival of Gary Bartlett. He was another Peace Corps Volunteer stationed in Kumba, about 25 miles away on the other side of Mt. Cameroon. I didn't like Gary very much. He was a braggart. He planned to go to veterinary school when he got home and had already applied to several colleges in the hope that if he were accepted before his two-year Peace Corps service was over, his draft board wouldn't have time to rescind his deferment.

Traveling volunteers usually sought out other volunteers and stopped to pass on news and talk about potato chips and Thanksgiving and lobster dinners. Most of the time I was happy to have a Peace Corps friend visit but in the case of Gary, I hoped he wasn't planning to stay too long. He wasn't. He'd just come by to brag.

Over our two cups of Nescafe, by the nice blue light of the

Tillie lamp, he told me that the next day he would be consulting with the Warden of the prison farm about the pigs.

"What pigs?" I asked.

Gary told me there'd just been a shipment of pigs to the farm from England. An experiment. The British advisor to the Minister of Agriculture figured the dairy cows had been such a success, maybe the prisoners could do as well with pigs. An alternate source of protein. Meat.

"People won't eat pork here, Gary. They're mostly Moslems."

"Well, I know, but it will be a good career opportunity for me."

"What will?"

"The pigs need to be castrated."

I put my cup down. "You're going to castrate a herd of pigs?"

"Not a herd, Maureen. Twelve."

"But why?"

"To make them grow big and fat."

"But why should they be big and fat if no one will eat them? And won't they need a lot of food themselves? What will the prisoners feed them?"

"Not my problem. My problem is to eliminate the pigs' sex drive."

He leered at me and winked, eliminating my sex drive. Why don't you just wink at the pigs, Gary, I thought. Instead, I asked, "Do you know how to castrate a pig?"

"Sure. You just cut into the sack, clip out the testicles, and stitch 'em up."

I didn't really want to hear how, just whether he could do it. "You've performed this operation before?"

"Well . . ."

"You've seen it done before?"

"Well . . ."

"Are you crazy, Gary?"

"Animal husbandry was my concentration at school. I'll get a great reference from the British agricultural advisor."

Elizabeth Ebenego walked in my front door. She'd dropped in because she saw my lamp on so late and wondered why. Cameroonians are curious people. She stopped short at the sight of Gary. He stood up to shake her hand. She glanced at me and a warm pleased look suffused her face before she modestly lowered her head scarf over her brow. She was worried about my prospects for marriage since I was 22 and past my prime. Elizabeth had a husband. He was studying economics in Moscow.

I said, "This is Gary Bartlett—Elizabeth Ebenego. Gary's here from St. Bonaventure's in Kumba."

"Pleased to make your acquaintance."

Gary said, "Same here." He smiled and looked into her eyes. Elizabeth reached up and lowered her scarf a little more. Cameroonian women become embarrassed when men look into their eyes. Cameroonian men don't do that to women. It's an offensive gesture. But women are fairly used to white men doing that to them.

"I have to be on my way," Gary said. "I've been saving my pennies for a night at the Buea Mountain Hotel with the British tea growers and those Danish sandwiches." Hans, the manager of the hotel was a Dane. "A shower," Gary went on, "and canned—tinned—peaches. Can't wait. Nice to meet you, Elizabeth. Bye, Maureen."

He left. Elizabeth said, "He is not a beau, is he?"

"He's a jerk."

"Ah, ah, ah," she said. "You say all these young Peace Corps men are jerks."

"Not all. Just a few. Especially that one."

We laughed. She said, "This word 'jerk' is a very curious word."

The next night at sundown I heard a knocking at the door. White person. Cameroonians don't knock. I hoped it wasn't one of the tea growers looking to invite me to some foolish British curry lunch or something.

It was Gary.

He looked horrible. His eyes were bulging out of his head,

his face was white and he was dripping sweat. I pulled him in.

"What's the matter with you?"

He burst into tears. I put my arms around him and he cried on my shoulder. Things have to be pretty bad for a jerk to cry. When he stopped crying he slumped down into my chair. I got him a beer. He said, "I'm so sick of warm beer."

But he drank it all. Then he said, "The pigs are dead. All of them."

"What happened?"

"I killed them."

"You killed them?" I pictured the pigs bleeding profusely from their balls.

"I over medicated them. They all ODed."

That was the funniest thing I'd ever heard. But I didn't laugh. I said, "Are they mad at you? The prisoners?"

"They don't know the pigs are dead. No one does. I told the guards they were sleeping and to leave them alone until the anesthesia wore off. Then I left. The anesthesia will never wear off."

"Gary, the prison people will eventually realize this."

"I know, but I just didn't know how to handle it. The pigs are all lying on tables with tubes hanging out of their legs. But they're dead."

"Did you castrate them?"

"Yes. When I got to the seventh one I thought he felt cold and wasn't bleeding much. But I finished the job and then I left."

"You castrated dead pigs?"

"Some."

"I think we need help. This could cause an international incident."

He looked up at me pathetically. "Do you think so?"

"Just trying to make a joke." What a jerk.

I told Gary to sit tight and ran down the road to Elizabeth's house. Her father and her mother and her father's other two wives and her brothers and sisters gathered around me. I asked them to come to my house because I needed help. We all trooped back, wrestled each other through my little front door, and sat on the floor looking at Gary. I told them what he'd done.

Elizabeth's father said, "This man has killed the swine. How fine."

The Ebenegos were Moslems.

"But he has a lot of trouble now, Mr. Ebenego. What should he do?"

"First he must go to the Warden and own up. Then he must make reparation for the slaughtered swine and all will be settled."

"How much, Gary?"

Gary whined, "Two thousand dollars."

"For twelve pigs!"

Elizabeth's father's senior wife said, "The swine are very dear. I don't know why."

Neither did I.

Mr. Ebenego said, "We will go see the Warden to settle this once and for all."

Mr. Ebenego was always using American expressions like "own up" and "once and for all" because he has an MBA from Penn State. Though he loved the United States, he is the Assistant Minister of Finance which is an important job and he has a large family so he doesn't have much hope of going back to Pennsylvania. This sometimes makes him melancholy so he often says to me, "Thank Allah for you Peace Corps."

The Warden welcomed us and insisted on refreshments. We all had warm beer and the kids had orange Crush, pronounced Croosh, a soda pop from England. Then we made our way to the operating room which was a big calving shed. I was carrying the baby of the junior wife. The presence of babies at all third world functions, crises, meals, parties, etc., kept people from acting frantic and made a lot of sense to me. Baby Luna was sleeping peacefully on my shoulder. The pigs looked like they were sleeping too, but they weren't. Each was on a table on a white tablecloth. They were pretty big.

The Warden said, "I see that there exists two difficulties here: One, our young friend must pay the British for his error. Perhaps the US Department of State could give him aid."

I whispered to Gary, "I don't think Dean Rusk will take your call." He glared at me.

The Warden went on, "Second, we must do something about the swine corpses before deterioration sets itself into the flesh."

He paused.

"I believe I have an idea."

We all looked to him hopefully.

"We must get in touch with that Negro Peace Corps fellow down at the Bonjongo Technical School who comes to teach us our maths on Monday evenings."

"Stonewall?" Gary and I said.

Stonewall Jackson Green from very rural Georgia. He taught math and he and his students also built a bar in Bonjongo-town when the original bar burned down. The townspeople named it "The President Kennedy Bar" as a tribute to Stonewall.

The Warden said, "This Stonewall told me he was once a poor dirt farmer before he became educated at University. I believe a U.S. dirt farmer would know what to do about dead swine."

I gave the baby to Gary. "I'll go call Stonewall."

Three prisoners escorted me to the telephone in the Warden's quarters. One prisoner said, "We are grateful we do not have to raise swine. They are foul beasts."

I smiled sadly at them. "But someone must pay reparations. Two hundred thousand francs."

"That is too bad," said one of the prisoners.

"I know."

I was put through to the Director of the Technical School. "Mr. Agbara, this is an emergency call for Stonewall Greene."

"Oh. An emergency, you say. I will procure him posthaste."

Posthaste took ten minutes as Stonewall was down at the President Kennedy Bar. He finally came to the phone, "Na who be dat?"

I said, "Stonewall, don't talk pidgin. This is Maureen."

"Which one?"

"The closest. In Buea."

There were four Maureens in our group. When we arrived in the country the Prime Minister greeted us by saying with a broad grin, "I have asked the U. S. for forty Peace Corps and they send four Marines." He laughed all over himself. Being one of the Maureens, I didn't think it was that funny.

"What's up, Yankee?"

I told him. I thought I heard a crafty chuckle.

"What do you think, Stonewall?"

"I think this weekend we are going to have a hell-fire Georgia barbecue to raise funds for the prisoners'. . . ah . . . let's see . . . the prisoners' health facility."

"They already have one."

"You can never have too much health. Call the hotel. Tell Hans the Peace Corps is having a fund raiser Saturday. Fill in the details. Meanwhile, I'm coming up to Buea right now. Take me half an hour. Don't touch those pigs."

I put a call through to Hans. He asked me, "What will you be wanting me to serve?"

"You get some chickens for the Buens, Hans, and all the rest of us will be having barbecued ribs and pork chops and pig knuckles . . . and picnic hams!"

"But I understood from a fellow who was here last night that although we could expect such a feast, it wouldn't be for some time. He told us in rather a crude way that first he'd have to cut off the privates of the pigs."

"That fellow accidentally killed the pigs during the crude operation. We'll be eating them on Saturday. Charge all the ministers and the tea growers a big wad of money."

"I will. But first I will attend to my refrigerators."

I went back to the calving shed and then Stonewall arrived with a big butcher knife. He licked his lips. He said, "Let me at those pigs."

Took Stonewall all night. Gary too. Stonewall made Gary dig a big hole for the pig parts that you don't eat.

Three hundred people came to our barbecue. Stonewall made barbecue sauce out of a crate of Hunt's Tomato Paste, beer, and honey from the Buea bee man. Those pigs tasted better than anything I'd ever had to eat before.

We danced the high-life the whole night through.

At five a.m., Mr. Ebenego, his second wife (Elizabeth's mother), the Warden, Stonewall, Hans, Gary, and Elizabeth and I sat at a table in the hotel garden under a Cinzano umbrella. We watched the early morning mists dissipate as the sun rose. The peak of Mt. Cameroon loomed into sight above us. I surprised everyone with a bottle of Old Grand Dad that my Granddad had sent me on my birthday. We raised our glasses to the mountain, no toast necessary as we couldn't help but feel overcome by the grandeur of the scene.

All of us that is except Gary.

"I guess we should drink to me. We'd never have had such a great party if it weren't for Mrs. Bartlett's cute little son."

So we had to drink to Gary.

Elizabeth winked under her lowered scarf and whispered to me, "I am now understanding the meaning of this word, jerk."

Mary-Ann Tirone Smith

Mary-Ann Tirone Smith was born in Hartford, Connecticut and graduated from Central Connecticut State University in 1965. She served as a Peace Corps Volunteer from 1965-67 in Buea, Cameroon, 5000 feet up the side of 14,000-foot Mt. Cameroon, an active volcano rising out of the equatorial African sea. Buea, where she organized West Cameroon's first public library, is the setting for her story, "Gary and the Pigs."

Smith has published three novels:
> *The Book of Phoebe*
>> (1985 Doubleday)
> *Lament for a Silver-Eyed Woman*
>> (1987 Morrow)
> *The Port of Missing Men*
>> (1989 Morrow and 1990 Fawcett paperback edition)

An occasional contributor to the *New York Times Book Review*, Smith is a member of PEN and the Author's Guild, and a volunteer in the PEN Literacy Program. *Lament for a Silver-Eyed Woman*, she believes, is "the first novel in which the author and main characters are Peace Corps Volunteers."

Smith is to be included in an as yet unpublished work by Shirley Jordan, Professor of English, Hampton University. In a series of interviews 12 black American women writers and 12 white American women writers will discuss, among other topics, the way they create fictional protagonists who belong to races different from their own. In addition to Smith, four of the other writers included are Josephine Humphreys, Tillie Olsen, Shirley Ann Williams and Alice Walker. The book will be published in 1992 by the Rutgers University Press.

Smith lives in Connecticut where she teaches a writing seminar at Fairfield University. She has recently completed a novel tentatively entitled, *Inside a Wife*, which takes place in four hours, "as opposed to my usual 25 years."

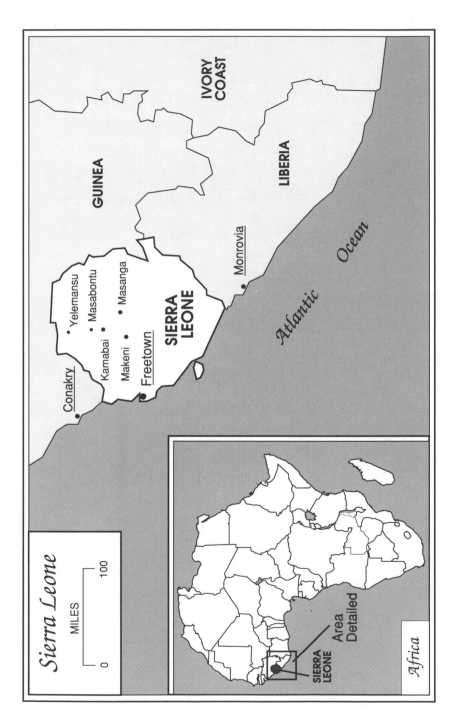

FODAY

William McCauley

I worked my way through the market to the hut of a trader who had a few bottles of beer on a shelf. I put twenty leones on the wood counter and asked for a Star. He popped the top off a dusty bottle and I took it and leaned back on the counter and drank the warm beer and observed the movement of people around a *poda-poda* parked on the road shoulder a few yards away. It was a Mazda one-ton flatbed, a banged-up, snub-nosed wreck of a truck that leaned heavily to the right. It had wood sides and benches and a sheet metal top on which there was a carrier piled high with baskets and boxes and ties of firewood. It was painted all over with religious slogans. The driver stood at the back, shouting at passengers to press inward so that another of the three dozen people waiting on the road could crowd in.

The trader said something to me and I turned to face him across the counter.

"*Pis-coh, notoso?*" he said. He was young, with the thin lips and small face of a Fullah.

I told him yes, in Freetown.

"*Pis-coh done help Salone beaucoup,*" he said, to please me. "*You saby dem pis-coh dem way dey na Masanga?*"

He mentioned the names of two volunteers who worked at the leprosy hospital and I nodded, saying yes, I knew them.

After that we talked for a while about how difficult things had become, he with a long face and helpless gestures, and then the conversation turned to the availability of petrol. He asked me if there was any in Freetown. I told him the only petrol coming in now was smuggled across the border from Guinea. And he knew that, better than I; he was merely flattering me, leading up to an offer for my five-gallon rubber of petrol. I told him it wasn't for sale. He offered 400 leones per gallon, and I turned him down again. We talked for a while longer, but I was nervous about not being near my bike, restless to be on the move again, so I ended our conversation and walked back the way I'd come.

The highway along the market was strewn with mango pits and the skins of oranges sucked dry. In the bushpole stalls of Fullah traders there were plastic half-backs, heaps of used clothing, mosquito coils, rice, kerosene. Market women squatted behind displays of mangoes, oranges, palm oil in stoppered Coke bottles, bananas, okra, casada, red peppers, bundles of potato leaf. Fish mammies from the coast offered baskets of dried bonga and herring.

The air possessed a rainy season clarity. In the east mares' tails swept down from thunderheads, but they were distant and more eastward than I was traveling and it was unlikely that I'd run under them. I retied the waterproof bag and the petrol rubber behind the saddle and headed north through the town. Within minutes I was in the bush on a dirt road. The lowland swamps were miles behind me; ahead was the savannah. The road curved over long stretches of rolling bush, a terrain of flats and swells that was pierced from time to time by anomalous rocky hills that jutted up sharply, and over which low clouds curled and rolled. In low places where streams flowed patches of swamp showed the emerald flatness of rice paddies. Clusters of mud and wattle houses surrounded by hardpacked earth appeared at the road edge every few miles, houses that erupted with children who ran waving to the edge of the road, their shouts lost in the whine of the bike.

A bike punishes you on a dirt road. It doesn't drive itself, as on blacktop; it has to *be* driven, and alertly, or it will go down over a pocket of sand or in an unexpected gully. And the saddle is uncomfortable, particularly in the rainy season when the air is humid. It's not made for long hauls, so your ass hurts, your balls and dick go numb, and because you're fighting the road, your arms tire, and you become a little dazed, and impatient, and then careless.

I made myself take the time to stop every hour or so at some place between villages where there were trees for shade. I'd remove goggles and helmet and gloves, shrug out of pack straps, adjust my sweat-wet underwear, and then I'd take the tire patch kit from my pack and roll a joint from the loose jamba and stretch out and smoke for a while and think of Susan; and I'd drink some water and watch the clouds and feel the energy seep back into my body with the high.

"What's wrong?" I asked.

"Oh, Paul, I'm so glad to see you," Susan said. She rose from the bed where she'd been sitting in her faded terry cloth bathrobe, crying. Wiping her face with her hands, she came to me and threw her arms around me. Her eyes were puffy and her hair was stringy and wet.

"What's happened?" I asked.

She drew a jerky breath. "It's Foday. He's gotten worse and I don't know what to do. I'm afraid he's going to die."

While I took off my muddy boots she told me he'd been improving, that he was eating and had shown interest in the picture books I'd sent and had been asking about me. And then, three days before, she'd taken food to him and found him hot and dazed, with his leg puffing up again. Since then the swelling and the fever had grown worse and he wouldn't eat.

"Let's go see him," I said.

"In a while. I'm going to wake him and try to get him to eat some rice pap."

"Are *you* taking care of him now?"

She nodded.

"What about that Sherbro nurse, and Doctor Shiaka? And the new dispenser, what's his name?"

"There's no petrol, so Shiaka never comes anymore, and

Isatu's gone back to Bonthe. And of course Williams hasn't been paid either, so he only shows up to steal drugs to sell in Magburaka or Makeni."

"There's no one at the dispensary?"

"It's locked up."

I rose and went to the kitchen and got a bottle of water and a plastic cup and came back into the room that served as Susan's bedroom and living room. In the third room of her house she stored her Honda and the head pans and shovels she loaned to farmers for digging the fish ponds.

"All I've done for days is look after Foday," she said. "He's been getting sicker and sicker. I don't know what I'm doing. I'm glad you came."

"I'm glad, too. I think about you all the time."

She smiled and her face brightened a little. She asked me how things were in Freetown. I told her it was still tense, but there was no disorder. We talked for a while longer about the petrol shortage and the inflation and the unavailability of currency and how our friends upline were dealing with it. And then I got up from the chair and went to her and leaned over her, putting my hands over her shoulders on the back of the chair and putting my face into hers. She had drawn her feet up, and she looked small and young and very appealing, even with her face coarsened by red and puffy eyes. I kissed her.

"I want to bathe," I said. "Join me."

She smiled. "I've already bathed," she said. "But I'll get you some water."

We went outside. While she took a bucket and went to the barrel of water at the end of the porch I took the petrol rubber and the waterproof bag into the house. Then I went to the spare room and got the long board Susan used as a ramp and wheeled my bike onto the porch, then into the house.

We locked the door and carried the bucket of water down the slope behind the house to the cotton tree. Beside it the villagers had built Susan a bathing *baffa* and not far away, a latrine. We talked while I stripped and bathed, dipping the brownish water with a plastic cup. I enjoyed her eyes on me so I took my time, soaping and rinsing twice, feeling the cool water drive out the jitteriness that remained in me from the long drive, leaving me full of a pleasant calm.

Darkness came, but the air remained hot and thick. Off to the east the pink tops of thunderheads were turning purple and were lit inside by flickers of lightning. Low rumbles reached us from time to time, the sound carried on a breeze that had sprung up from the east. A band of red lingered above the western horizon and the hills and valleys were dark.

I dressed in clean clothes and ran a comb through my hair. We walked back up the slope to her house, which was round with mud walls and thatch roof in the Mandingo style, and got the rice pap and a bottle of water and walked on into the village. Behind the round houses high wattle fences protected garden plots from goats. The gardens had been freshly raked into mounds that bristled with starter twigs of casada and green sprigs of sweet potato cuttings.

We greeted people sitting on porches and they waved and shouted greetings back to us. Two girls came out of a group of children playing beside one of the houses and approached us. They were in their early teens, with bare upright breasts and plump faces and hair done up into scores of small, tight braids. They wore lapas and plastic half-backs. The tallest of the two carried a naked baby on her hip.

"Susan, how de pikin? 'E done bet-tah?" she asked. She looked curiously at me.

"No, he done make sick beaucoup."

"Osha," the girls murmured, and fell into step with us. They looked sidelong at me again. Then, grinning, the tall one whispered to Susan, *"Na you man, notoso?"*

Susan curled her arm around mine. *"Yes-o. Na me man."*

The girls giggled.

"The one with the baby is Ebun, and the other is Mamuna," Susan said to me. "They've helped me take care of Foday."

The two girls went with us to the dispensary. We went round to the outbuilding in back, which was divided into two rooms. Susan turned on her flashlight and the beam went to the bed, then it flicked about the room, before coming back to the bed.

"Damn," she murmured.

I was behind her. "What's the matter?"

"The lantern's gone." She turned to Ebun. *"You saby who done tief de lantern?"*

Ebun and Mamuna shook their heads.

I approached the bed and turned on my flashlight and aimed it at the wall above Foday's head and looked at him in the reflected light. The dingy sheet was off him and his night shirt was pulled up to his stomach, exposing his legs and genitals. He was as small as a five-year-old, thin and bony except for his right leg, which was large and hot and swollen up as tight as a cooked sausage. The wounds around his ankles and wrists were bandaged. I moved the light so that I could see his face. His eyes were slits; I could only sense that he was awake and that he watched me.

"Foday, how de go de go?"

He didn't move.

Susan was at my side, holding the plastic bowl and the other flashlight.

"What's Williams given him for the infection?" I asked.

"Tetracycline. It's all we have. But Williams hasn't been here for days."

"His leg looks bad. He needs antibiotics. I'll go get another lantern and my tools. I'm gonna get in the dispensary."

When I got back she was sitting on the edge of Foday's bed, trying to get him to eat. Ebun and Mamuna lingered by the door, watching. I tried to help by holding him up, but it was no use. All he took was a little water. I stood back out of the way and watched as Susan bathed him.

Afterwards we went outside and walked round to the front of the dispensary. With a tire iron I broke the lock on the front door and we went into the examination room, which contained a table, chairs, and a tall cabinet, the doors of which were secured by a padlock. It took just a moment to break the hasp.

We swung the doors open and directed our flashlight beams at the shelves of medicines and drugs and instruments. Neither of us knew what we were looking for, so we proceeded slowly along each shelf, from tray to tray, looking at labels. There were bottles of aspirin and Aralen, bandages, lozenges, rehydration packets, ointments, salves, disinfectants. I found the tray containing a few small boxes of tetracycline, but the instructions on the boxes were in French, so I couldn't understand anything but the tablet size. We took a box and closed the cabinet and went back outside. While I waited on the porch, Susan went back to her house to get one of her padlocks to replace the one I'd broken, and her volume of *Where There Is No Doctor*.

The wind came now in cool gusts that swirled dust into the air and the thunder had become a continuous rumble, punctuated by cracks like rifle shots. In the lightning's flickering whiteness I watched Susan walking, as if under erratic strobes, back across the open space around the court *bari*.

While I repaired the hasp and installed the new lock on the door Susan leafed through the book by the light of her flashlight. After some discussion we crushed a few tablets and dissolved the powder in some sugar and water and took it inside to Foday.

While Susan coaxed him to drink the mixture I stood in the door, looking out at the sky.

"Paul, I think we ought to take Foday to my house and take care of him there."

I looked over my shoulder at her. "Yeah, I agree. In the morning I'll drive to Makeni and see if I can get one of the sisters to come for him in a Land Rover. I'll take the petrol, in case they're low."

"Yes," she said, still holding Foday's head near her breast, coaxing him to drink from the plastic cup.

We moved the table and chairs into the extra room with the bikes and the tools and put Foday's mattress in the place where the table had been, under the window. We took his temperature. It was over 104. We rinsed his body with cool water, but it made him uncomfortable, so we stopped. We tried twice to get him to take some aspirin and sugar water, but most of it ended up on his shirt. Finally, he closed his eyes and sank exhausted into sleep. There was nothing more to do so we went outside to the porch of the round Mandingo house and sat on the top step.

I realized that we hadn't eaten. Susan said she had some

tins of sardines and there was rice left over from the morning. So, sitting on the porch, we ate the oily sardines out of tins and the sticky, cold rice out of the pot and talked about how good a beer would taste, and I regretted not buying a couple more from the Fullah trader. When we finished I went inside and got my tire patch kit and brought it back out to the porch and we smoked some jamba and savored the coolness coming with the gusting wind. The thunder had become a series of overlapping cracks and booms that trailed off to echoing rumbles, and from time to time lightning would stab down close by and we would hear the whispering click of it, followed instantly by a ripping explosion that surged over us like a wave in heavy surf. The storm lit the open space between Susan's round Mandingo house and the village with a flickering whiteness, and the rain came first in big drops that thudded against the red earth before the porch and then it came roaring like a waterfall.

We rose a couple of times in the night to check on Foday. His temperature remained high and his breathing was shallow. He opened his eyes when we tried to give him aspirin and tetracycline, but there was little awareness in him.

I was outside before first light tying the petrol rubber to the bike when Susan screamed for me. I ran inside. She stood trembling in the candle light over Foday's mattress. The flashlight was at her feet, it's beam shining a path across the cement floor toward her bed. Her face was pinched and her hands were clenched together and pressed into her stomach.

I directed the beam of my flashlight to Foday's face. His mouth had sagged open. I knelt beside him and put my ear to his chest. His skin was cool, his flesh silent. My first thought was CPR, and I even made the first motions—putting my fingers in his mouth and pulling his tongue forward—but I realized it would not change anything and I drew back. For several seconds I squatted there beside the mattress, looking down at him, thinking I ought to do something but not knowing what to do. Then I rose and took Susan's arm and led her outside.

It was just full light, with the sun still below the horizon, when the village headman and several other men of the village met at the court *bari*, ostensibly to arrange the transport of Foday's body to his grandmother in Yelemansu. They went through the motions of discussion, but it ended in a big *hala-hala*. Who would pay for it? Who would be responsible? And how was it to be done, with public transport no longer coming to Masabontu? Foday was a Susu; he had no kin in Masabontu; he was not the responsibility of Masabontu village.

Foday had lived with his grandmother in Yelemansu, some 20 miles to the north, not far from the Guinea border. She and one of her sons had brought Foday to the dispensary six weeks before, too weak to walk, with open wounds on his wrists and ankles. They had walked the 20 miles, Foday on the back of his uncle.

Isatu, the nurse, was still there then, resentfully doing as little of her duty as possible. She had not been paid for five months. She put Foday in a bed, bandaged his wrists and ankles, allowed the grandmother to sleep on the floor of his room, and abandoned him. She passed the time on the porch of the dispensary plaiting the hair of one or another of the young women of the village, or having her own hair plaited, and telling those who came for medicine that they would have to see Williams.

Foday's grandmother inflicted his wounds. She'd tied him, hands and feet, for days at a time, to keep him from running off to find his father, who worked in Freetown. The rough cord had chafed his skin raw and open sores had developed, which became ulcerated, then infected. She was not evil, not angry, not hateful; she was merely stupid, and probably crazy.

Susan took over caring for Foday. She paid one of the village women to prepare food for him and his grandmother, and she cleaned him and changed his bandages. After ten days his grandmother became restless and left, promising to come for him soon.

And so it was natural that the matter of taking Foday home, like the responsibility for taking care of him, fell to Susan.

After paying the carpenter to make a coffin, I tied the petrol rubber to my bike and drove the ten miles of rutted and gullied trail out to the Makeni road at Kamabai. There among the bushpole market stalls scattered along the main road through town I looked for a *poda-poda* to hire to take Foday back to his village. I found one vehicle discharging passengers, but the driver would not even talk to me when he learned where I wanted him to go. I waited an hour before a second truck arrived at the market. It was a tired, badly used Toyota pickup with wood benches along both sides of an extended box beneath a canvas top. I approached the driver, a 20-year-old who stood off to the side polishing his teeth with a twig as he watched his assistant, a boy Foday's age, help passengers clamber down from the box with their baskets and bundles. I told him that I wanted to hire his *poda-poda* to transport the body of a young boy.

He looked me over, then removed the twig and sucked his teeth and spat off to the side. *"Usai de pikin?"*

"Masabontu, wey he done die. We get for carry am go for Yelemansu."

He shook his head. *"No possible. Na wo-wo road."* He nodded at the truck. *"'E go 'poil."* He made as if to leave me.

I told him I would pay in petrol and he paused. *"How mos' petrol you get?"*

"Five gallon." I pointed toward my bike and the black petrol rubber tied behind the saddle.

He shook his head again.

"Pady, du-ya help we, I beg." I offered the petrol and a thousand leones. He thought about it for a moment, then shrugged, saying he would do it for the petrol and four thousand leones. We settled on three thousand, and then we argued some more when he demanded that I give him the petrol immediately. He complained that he would not have enough petrol unless he got what I had. I refused and he left off, saying irritably that he had to make some repairs before we could leave. I wandered into the market where I found a woman selling bean sandwiches. After eating I came back to the *poda-poda* to find the driver's assistant loading passengers. The driver was sweating under the hood of the truck.

"We no go able for carry dem passenger dem go," I said angrily, pointing to the passengers at the rear of the truck. *"I done pay you*

for carry de coffin go foh Yelemansu. Leh we go. Now."

"*For bear,*" he said crossly, from under the hood. "*We no de carry beaucoup pohsin go.*" He pointed to the rear of the truck. "*Look am.*"

"No more," I yelled angrily.

In a half hour, with a full load of passengers, we were on our way out of town.

The truck pulled into the open space at the court *bari* and stopped. Villagers suddenly appeared in the court *bari* and on the porches of nearby houses. Several waved at me as I turned the bike in a circle, stopping at the driver's door of the *poda-poda*.

"*Wait small,*" I said. "*I de come just now.*" Then I drove across the open space to Susan's house. Her knapsack was on the porch. The door was open and she came out as I drove up.

"You okay?" I said.

"I'm okay." She put her arms around me. "I'm gonna have to write a report about this for Max. Williams came a couple of hours ago. We had hell of a *palavah*. He's going to make trouble with the ministry about our breaking in the dispensary. He wasn't inside ten seconds before he came out and started yelling about drugs being *tiefed*. He's gonna use the break-in to cover his ass. He wants money."

"Fuck 'im," I said.

"He's gonna make trouble for you, too."

"Fuck 'im."

"He's with Pa Sesay in the court *bari*, waiting to see you."

"I'm not gonna talk to him. Did the carpenter finish?"

"Yes. They took Foday and put him in the coffin. He's over by the court *bari*." Her arms tightened around me. "Oh, Paul, I don't want to go to Yelemansu, I just want to go to Freetown and stay with you and lay on the beach and eat good food and not think about anything."

"We will. But first we have to take Foday home."

We went inside. Susan poured me a cup of water and I drank it down, then looked around the room. The netting over the bed was up, the bed was made, my waterproof bag rested on the floor beside the bed. Foday's mattress was gone and the table and chairs were back in their places below the window.

The shutters were unlatched and ready to be closed and secured to the iron bars.

"I had a half-gallon of petrol in my bike," she said. "I drained it into a rubber." She pointed to the plastic anti-freeze container by the door.

"We'll need it," I said.

"We could stop at Masanga and see if Carol or Reed have any."

"They'll need what they have. I think we should just go on to Makeni and stay in the resthouse until tomorrow, then beg some from the Brits over at Bridges and Ferries. Oliver'll give me a couple of gallons, if they've got it."

While I tied my bag down Susan put her petrol into my Honda. I drove the Honda back across the open space to the court *bari* while Susan locked her house.

The passengers had climbed down from the *poda-poda* and joined the villagers in the shade of the court *bari*. The driver was under the hood of the truck. He closed it and wiped his hands on a rag as I came up.

"*I done load am,*" he said.

We went to the back of the *poda-poda*. The coffin was a small box, fashioned from faded boards. It rested on the floor between the two benches. The driver explained that it was not necessary to tie it down. It would not move about after the passengers and their baggage were loaded. When I looked dubious, he snapped, "*E go do.*"

"*I tink say we get foh tie am pan de bench.*"

"*I no get rope,*" he said irritably.

I untied the petrol rubber and my bag and used the rope to tie the coffin to the bench on one side. Then we put the petrol rubber and the waterproof bag in the back of the truck.

While we secured the coffin and loaded the passengers Susan stood a few paces away, talking to the headman. When we finished I shook hands with the headman and those around him. I had seen Williams come out of the court *bari* and stand off to the side while I worked with the driver securing the coffin. As Susan and I went to the bike he crossed the open space toward us.

I had my gloves and helmet on, and was swinging my leg over the seat as he came up. I kick-started the bike.

"Mr. Garrison," he said. "I am Mr. Williams, of the Ministry of Health. We must talk about the drugs you took."

"There's nothing to talk about," I said. I pulled my goggles down over my eyes and waited as Susan secured her helmet and climbed onto the bike behind me.

"Mr. Garrison, I am responsible for the drugs that are missing. They must be replaced or paid for."

I waved at the driver of the *poda-poda*. He put the pickup in gear and it edged forward, turning in a wide circle in the open space before the court *bari*, then moved between the houses, lurching and swaying ponderously as it turned onto the rutted track toward Yelemansu. Black faces looked out at me, faces that glistened with sweat and merged into shadows beneath the canvas top.

I glanced at Williams, who stood off to the side and just forward of the bike. He wore a soiled polyester safari suit and plastic half-backs. His hair was cropped short and there was gray along his temples. I knew he had walked ten or 15 miles that morning, and that he would walk another ten to get out to Kamabai with drugs to sell in Makeni. I was drawn to him for a moment, I suppose because I felt some of the humiliation of his scramble to stay alive and to feed his family. He sensed that empathy and he stepped to the side of the bike and put one hand on the handlebar beside my gloved hand.

"*Du-ya, I beg, Mr. Garrison. Leh we talk pan dis business.*"

The empathy dissolved and the wall rose; I was on my guard again. And just as I would not let him close enough to truly understand his humiliation, so he could not understand the effect of his words: he looked surprised when I said, "*You na tiefman, Williams. I no de gi' you notting.*" I put the bike in gear and released the clutch and felt Susan's arms tighten around my waist as the rear tire dug into the red dirt and the bike leaped forward.

William McCauley

Born in Oklahoma City of southern parents, William McCauley attended the University of Washington where he received a BS in geological oceanography in 1969. He continued to work with the University, traveling extensively as a marine technician until 1976, when he became self-employed.

From 1985-87, McCauley served with the Peace Corps in Tombo and Freetown, Sierra Leone, with the Fisheries Pilot Project Tombo (FPPT), a development project funded and managed by the West German government. His short story, "Foday," is drawn from his experiences in Sierra Leone. He has also traveled widely in Mexico and Europe.

Upon returning to the United States, McCauley completed a BS in scientific and technical communication at his alma mater. He has been employed as a senior technical writer in Kirkland and is a member of the Society of Technical Communication.

McCauley has had a story appear in *Confrontation*, a publication of Long Island University and is currently at work on another collection of short stories.

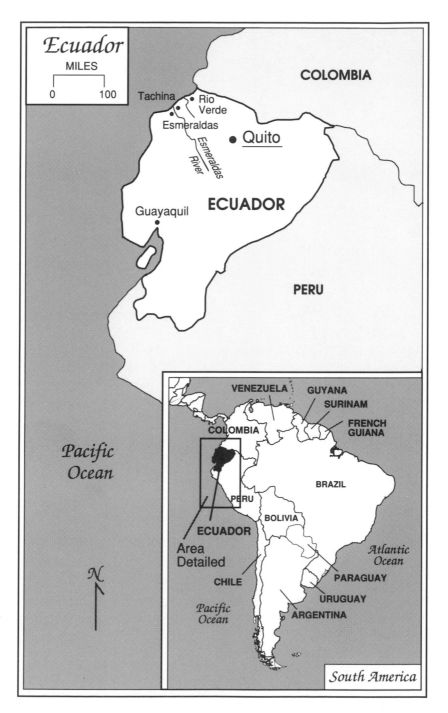

RAMON

Moritz Thomsen

Rio Verde, 1966

During my first weeks in Rio Verde, misunderstandings kept cropping up when I tried to speak Spanish in the village. Let me explain: my house had two rooms, all plaster, and a tin roof designed to collect rain water outside the bedroom window in a large cement barrel. I not only had the best house but the only sweet water, since the well in the street pumped brine, and most of the drinking water had to be hauled down the river in canoes.

At that time the back of my house was full of corn and chickens; they were separated by a narrow aisle in which I had put my bed. I slept there, rather tentatively, with a flashlight in one hand and several rocks in the other, the object being to be forever on tippy-toe alert and to scare the hell out of the rats when they swaggered in to kill the chicks. We had made a temporary deal, the rats and I; they could eat the corn as long as they left the chicks alone and as long as they entered nicely, in sedate twos and threes rather than as an unruly, brawling, bickering mob.

Rio Verde was a seacoast town, and there wasn't a house, of course, that wasn't cursed with rats. A bamboo wall was no challenge at all; a good self-respecting rat could walk through one without slowing down. I had awakened several times, my flesh crawling, with rats running across my legs or over my arms, and the kids told me that they must wash their hands after having eaten fish or the rats would chew on their fingers while they slept.

For whoever might come to visit me from the outside, I had borrowed another bed; it sat in my front room ready for instant occupation. I sometimes wished it were used more often, and apparently I was not the only one. I was talking to Jorge Avila after supper one evening out on the dock, where we would go to sit on benches, watch the sunset, and receive the first cool night winds from the ocean. Jorge was about twenty-one, unemployed along with everyone else in town; he made a few sucres carrying passengers across the river in his father's canoe or, at low tide, hauling tins of water to the different houses. Jorge was a nice guy, not funny and flashy like many of the young men, but very quiet, very stolid. He was invisible in a crowd, but when he got you alone he rambled on endlessly and earnestly in an incomprehensible flood of soft words. He spoke a very bad, lazy, coastal Spanish, made more than usually liquid by the absence of two front teeth.

"And isn't it sad for you, sleeping alone in that big house?" he asked me.

"No, it's not so bad," I said. "I sleep very *tranquilo*."

"But those bandits, those rats," he insisted. "It must be very bad being alone in the night when the rats come."

"Well, yes, I don't like the rat part very much."

"You need a companion," Jorge said. "Someone to sleep in the house with you, to keep you company."

"Yes, Jorge," I said, "that's what I need all right."

But it became apparent after about an hour that we were not talking about the same thing, because at eight o'clock, bedtime, as we were walking back down the street, Jorge called his brother over and told him that I was sad and that he was going to sleep in the house with me.

"Good," little brother Ricardo said. "I'll go get Jesús."

"Well, now look," I said. "I'm not *that* sad."

"It's no trouble at all," Jorge said. "It's sad to live alone, and we can be your companions and talk."

"And furthermore," Ricardo said, "I have never slept in a bed and have a great desire to sleep in one."

"You're a savage brute," Jorge said. "I have slept in a bed many times; once at the school in Conocoto I slept in a bed for more than a month."

Now, I can reconstruct this conversation; but at the time much of it was conjectural. I wasn't completely sure that I understood them—or whether they were serious if I *did* understand them. I finally left them talking in the street, went into the house, and got ready for bed. Getting ready for bed involved no more than watering the chicks, putting a kerosene lamp in their sleeping quarters, and pounding on the floor several times with a large stick to let the rats know that the old boy upstairs was still moving around vigorously.

I lay down just about the time there was a knock on the door. When I opened it, Jorge, Jesús, and Ricardo solemnly filed in and matter-of-factly marched across the room and stretched out on the spare bed. They all pretended to be very sleepy, yawning elaborately, but long after I had gone into the back room with the chickens and the rats, I could hear them talking. Mostly they were analyzing the fine quality of the bed and exclaiming over its great comfort—a bed made of wooden slats covered with a *petate* of woven vines. I woke up once and Jorge was telling them about his month in Conocoto and about the tremendous buildings in Quito—at least, that's what I think he was talking about—Jorge, the traveler to distant parts.

How any of them slept, I'll never know. Two of the kids were fully grown, and Ricardo, sort of a runty type, was fifteen years old; the bed was slightly larger than an army cot. But there they were in the morning, curled up like young fox cubs. I sat drinking the three or four cups of coffee I need to face another day, and one by one they awoke and drifted out of the house.

I thought that was the end of it until that night at bedtime when there was a knock on the door, and Jorge—very shy, very sweet—appeared, with a row of faces dimly visible in the darkness behind him.

"I've got Miguel and Ernesto this time," he said, "and of course, my brother, Ricardo; we've come to keep you company for the sadness of the rats."

"Thank you very much," I told him, beginning to laugh hysterically, "but truly, there isn't room for four of you, and furthermore I'm not sad any more. I think you scared the rats away last night."

I closed the door on four disappointed, unbelieving faces, and instead of going to bed, I studied Spanish verbs for half an hour.

Some people have a special feeling of accommodation when it comes to learning a foreign tongue; other people will forever blunder and stutter drunkenly, unable to make that first decisive change-over, to begin thinking in the language they are learning. I am one of the slow ones who hears a word a hundred times before it clicks into place.

For instance, Alexandro had a wild four-year-old daughter who was always showing off. "Grosera" the parents kept calling her; I thought it was her name. "Good morning, little Grosera," I'd say, only slightly put off when they called one of the boys "Grosero" from time to time. Then one day, in a brilliant burst of illumination, I realized that the word was sort of like "gross." Sure enough, in the dictionary *"grosera"* turned out to be a lout, a rude, crude, unpolished person.

Another example of my facility with Spanish: in Ecuador an introduction is a rather formal moment. You are presented to an Ecuadorian, who nicely says that he is absolutely enchanted to meet you and that he is at your service—*a sus órdenes*. For months I simply acknowledged these gracious speeches of pleasure by mumbling over and over, *"Mucho gusto, Señor, mucho gusto."* But later, bloated with a self-confidence that had no basis in reality, I began to reply with a few gracious comments of my own. *"A su servicio,"* I would say, smiling brightly and shaking my new friend's hand. *"A su servicio,"* at your service. Someone drew me aside one day and pointed out very discreetly that if I were saying anything at all, I was only offering a toast, "Here's to your bathroom," and that in many cases, particularly if the man had no bathroom, I might conceivably be treading on sensitive nerve endings.

The best, the only way to learn Spanish, everyone in the Peace Corps agreed, was to live in a village where only Spanish was spoken. Then as a matter of simple survival the words and phrases would live and harden in the mind. Up to a point it was true; in no time at all I could express the fundamentals. "To me it is very friendly and rich this fish them," I would say in impeccable Spanish, receiving a dazed smile of appreciation from my hostess. Or out on a jungle trail I had only to say,"I am almost dead of the drys and have somewhat of a great yearning for a wet thing," and from the nearest palm a coconut appeared, its top cut away to reveal the fresh, sweet milk.

But after I had polished up these fundamentals of survival, a basic frustration of communication still remained. I could only go so far with smiles, titters, slaps on the back, little grunts of amazement and pleasure, happy foot stampings and soft-shoe shuffles. This was fine for those superficial relationships that formed on a bus or in a store, but for the long haul—for the friendships which began to grow in my own village, in the house where I ate my meals, with the kids who swam with me almost every day—this inability to talk easily and deeply about ideas, convictions, prejudices was an infuriating thing. For we were, of course, very curious about one another, and we wished to probe each other to our own limits.

The limits of curiosity in some cases didn't go very deep. Most of the housewives in the village were fanatically interested mainly in the number of clothes I sent each week to the *señora's* to be washed, and they were scandalized by the number of cigarettes I smoked, but this was just the usual small-town stuff. It was slightly flattering to be so closely observed and to be the object of such intense interest until I realized that I was set apart, separated from the true life of the town. I had come to show them my best side, and this was what they wanted to show me, too. About the time the bad side started showing through—the hatred between particular families, the jealousies between disenchanted friends, my awareness of the town alcoholics—my own bad side was also coming to the front. And

201

when the kids started pounding on my door at five in the morning bumming paint for their tops, it was impossible not to use my wonderful new word and yell "Groseros!" at them through the still-locked door.

At the same time there would always exist a separation. After forty-five years Mister Swanson was still a gringo. Everyone knew how many beers he drank each day, how he made love, what he said the last time his son came to see him. You were separated by the color of your skin, that sickly paleness that in this country was so ugly as to be embarrassing. You were separated by your lousy Spanish, by the typewriter that sat on your table or the camera you sometimes packed around; you were separated from many by the simple fact that on the day you arrived you had the carpenter make you a bed— sleeping on a bed of wooden slats somehow indicated refinement, real sensibility. Even the fact that you didn't eat those horrible baked or boiled *plátanos* with every meal set you apart and made a sort of freak of you.

When Alexandro's wife introduced me to her mother, she said, "This is Don Martín; he won't eat *plátano* or *yuca*; he drinks two cups of coffee with every meal and smokes innumerable cigarettes." And the older woman, too amazed to even acknowledge the introduction, simply sat there slack-jawed trying to visualize a man who wouldn't eat *plátano*. It was just too unbelievable. All through the meal she squatted in one dark corner of the room watching me drink two cups of coffee, muttering to herself.

Occasionally, more often than it would seem possible, someone—a friend—would begin to appear out of the crowds of people with whom I lived and worked. There came a time when I realized that someone regarded me as just another human being rather than as an exotic curiosity. It was always miraculous when it happened. It was a break-through, a transcending of all the things that made us look at each other strangely or suspiciously.

We had been trained in the Peace Corps to see through, a little way at least, that cultural veneer to the common humanity that binds us together, but no one in Rio Verde had had that training. We were trained to give of ourselves, we were trained to overlook or partially understand the eccentricities of an alien culture. I don't remember that anything was ever said about receiving this same understanding.

"I think you're a good man; let's be brothers," Ramón Prado, the young fisherman, said to me as we sat eating oranges and talking by candlelight on a night of profound darkness, and it was said so naturally, so sweetly, that for a second the room actually blazed with light.

"Yes," I said, extremely moved, "let's be brothers."

But I wanted to say more; I felt deprived, almost idiotic, for it was a moment of great seriousness for both of us. "Yes, let's be brothers." For the time being, at any rate, that's all I had to know how to say; it was enough.

My first weeks in Rio Verde I talked to everyone in town and went up and down the beach blowing off to the tobacco farmers and the fishermen about chickens. They are the most expensive meat in Ecuador at forty cents a pound. With all the cheap corn and fish and a perfect climate, it seemed that the best way to dazzle the local people with the brilliance of the Peace Corps was to get some successful chicken projects going. There was enthusiasm for the idea of chickens, but the initial cost of bamboo, roof thatching, nails, and lumber represented almost prohibitive investments. I had a hundred chickens living in my bedroom; it would be time soon to distribute them, and so far there wasn't a single chicken coop in town.

I was sitting in my house drinking morning coffee when my new brother, Ramón, stopped by to visit. He was carrying a paddle.

"Where are you going?" I asked him.

"Up the river," he said. "I've been thinking and thinking about what you told us; I'm going up the river to buy bamboo. I've talked the whole thing over with my wife. If you'll draw me the plans for a *gallinero* I've decided to go in the chicken business."

Ramón was my first real live customer, the first guy in town with enough faith in me to take a chance. "Good," I said.

"That's great. I'll even help you build it; I'll donate the nails. Now tell me, what kind of chickens do you want, for eggs or for meat?"

He thought that over for a while and then very gravely told me, "About half and half, I think."

"That's a good idea," I said. "We'll have to divide the house down the middle. Then you can see which type makes the most money for you. Now, as I told you, the main thing is that you have enough money for a balanced ration. Without a balanced ration, without protein, this whole new system is worthless."

"Yes, I understand," he said.

"They have to have milled corn, fish meal and a vitamin supplement."

"Exactly," Ramón said.

"Good. Now how many chickens do you think you can afford to raise? We have to make the *gallinero* big enough, two and one half square feet for each chicken."

"Yes," Ramón said. "I want to do everything just right. I think I can handle six chickens—three for meat and three for eggs."

God, how I loved Ramón in that moment, for his innocence and for his honesty and for the modesty of his ambitions.

Just because I was Ramón's brother didn't, I discovered, make me a member of the family. Orestes, Ramón's oldest brother, started to hang around the house in the evenings. He was darkly silent and brooding around me, suspicious of the projects I talked about, half under the spell, I think, of the *Policía Rural*, who was convinced that I was an FBI spy and who, Ramón told me, was preaching this conviction in the town. "I don't know what is here, but there is something here, some great richness, some great national treasure, for why else would an *Americano* come to live in a town like this?"

Orestes was a *mocho*, someone who has lost part of his body— an arm, a leg, or in the case of Orestes, his fingers. "Mocho" was one of his nicknames, a name he loathed. He had never become reconciled to the maiming of his right hand, and this loss, perhaps more than anything, had poisoned his whole way of looking at life. Life for Orestes was pretty lousy, and so were all the people in it.

The day after Ramón went up the river for bamboo Orestes came to my house and said he wanted chickens, too. Unlike Ramón, who spoke with charm, Orestes was as blunt and clear as a bulldozer; he didn't know how to ingratiate himself with anyone and probably would have scorned such tactics. I drew up some plans for him, and he listened intently as I explained the spaces between the bamboo, but I was uncomfortable with him still and didn't offer to help him in the construction.

As he was leaving, he turned and showed me a face tight and drawn with some deep feelings of deprivation. "You have to help me build it, too," he said, not looking into my eyes. "You're going to help Ramón; you have to help me too."

"*Encantado*," I said. Enchanted. "Whenever you're ready, tell me."

"And is it true that you are buying the nails for Ramón?"

"Yes," I said. "I told Ramón I'd get the nails."

"Then I want you to buy me nails, too," he said staring bleakly at a spot on the floor.

It was amazing to compare the faces of the two brothers, faces which were almost identical in their features, and find such disparate qualities. Ramón's face was all delight, quickness, light. His humor was constant and a real part of his way of seeing things; life was a great joke in spite of everything. He was like a trick pony, quick on his legs, volatile, a real prancer. Orestes was a work horse. There wasn't a trick in him; he was built for the long pull. His sense of humor, unlike Ramón's, which was a bubbling over of youth and optimism (and many times quite foolish), was black, bitter, and profound. Everyone in town laughed with Ramón, he was so quick and lightly mocking. But no one laughed when Orestes spoke. His humor was much deeper and cutting. A couple of months after we built the chicken coops, when Orestes realized that I thought his jokes were something quite special, he began to like me. It was always hard to tell with Orestes, but it's almost impossible to dislike someone who thinks your jokes are bellybusters.

Finally the first one hundred Heifer-Peace Corps chickens were ready to sell to the farmers. I charged only for the feed and the vaccine that I had used raising them up to six weeks—about twenty-seven cents each. The magnificent squawkers weighed well over a pound, and after living in the same room with me they were extremely lovable creatures, although sort of domineering. I had enjoyed the close relationship, but I was glad to see them go. A few of them had seemed determined to peck my eyes out and had perched on the edge of my bed in the early mornings waiting for me to wake up. Wise to their tricks, I would lie there, eyes tightly shut, and think about Alfred Hitchcock.

Over a period of about three days the farmers arrived with baskets, and we loaded them up, each farmer picking out particular birds that he wanted in his flock. Finally, except for about six hundred pounds of chicken shit in my bedroom, nicely mixed with balsa shavings from the mill upstream, everything turned tranquil and placid around the house. I had kept the bottom chicken in the pecking order, a scrawny bird named Condor, and he continued to live in the house with me. He was the sweetest chicken I ever knew, a true friend who would wail and cry whenever I left him alone, and rush into my arms when called, moaning with ecstasy. Every kid in town wanted Condor, and finally the pressure was too great; I gave him to Miguel, my favorite, who built a special chicken house for him on a high bluff overlooking the ocean.

I had browbeaten Ramón into building a house for twelve chickens, but he was a little nervous starting out so big. I got a terrific pleasure out of working with Ramón because he was so enchanted with the things we built. His chicken house looked the same as everyone else's, but he never tired of talking about how beautiful it was, how much prettier than the others. I visited him three days after he had taken the chickens home and found that he had made little balsa-wood shades for the feed and water. He and his wife Esther spent their free time petting the chickens and lifting each one up to exclaim over its great weight.

I visited the other chicken projects, and there seemed to be no problems. This was a relief, because a week before the distribution the local chickens running free and wild in the town had all come down with cholera and most of them were dead. Nobody was worrying about the gringo chickens catching cholera because "they were vaccinated chickens." When I explained that they were vaccinated only against Newcastle and not cholera, there was no reaction. Nothing could happen to those great-footed, magnificent creatures.

Everything was fine for a couple of weeks, and then Ramón rushed into town one morning to tell me that one of his chickens was picking all the tail feathers out of the others. He was very worried. Some of the chickens had bloody rear ends. "You'll have to separate the chicken right away," I told him. He went home and put the outlaw chicken in the house, tied by a piece of vine to the leg of a stool. The next morning he was back; another chicken in the group was madly pecking out tail feathers.

"Don't panic, " I said. "You'll have to separate this one too." Within five days he had separated five chickens; they were tied in the kitchen, outside under palm trees, under the steps. Ramón had a harried look, and he came in one day utterly defeated; all the chickens were pecking each other's tail feathers. "Oh my God," he said, "I don't want my chickens to die."

I read up on debeaking. We went out and used a red-hot wood chisel to cut and burn a piece of beak from the neurotic creatures. All through the operation Ramón was distraught. I was killing his chickens; I was cutting off too much; I was making them suffer. They looked sort of stupid with their beaks cut off, and I made the mistake of laughing at their appearances. Ramón was furious with me. "You're really enjoying yourself, aren't you?" he would ask me after each hen had gone through her ordeal, giving me the cold glance of total rejection. When we had debeaked ten of the twelve he told me that that was all, meaning, I found out later, that that was all he could stand for one day.

Before that Ramón used to come by the house almost every evening, along with other of my friends, and visit for a few minutes, but he didn't show up for several days. He sat in the doorway of his salon across the street, tilted against the wall, staring at the palm trees. On some days he probably didn't sell more than half a dozen cigarettes and a Siete Oop—which means Seven Up, just in case your Castilian is a little rusty. I would stop by to ask him about the chickens, but he was in a depression, a sort of shock, and he would begin his sentences with expressions like, "If it is God's will." The chickens weren't eating, he told me. How could they, poor creatures? "And you're right, they are sort of ugly."

"But almost every chicken in the United States is debeaked," I said. "Just keep more feed in the bamboo."

"All they eat is the corn, the poor little ones; they can't eat the concentrate, it's too fine."

"You'll have to grind the corn finer, is all."

"Yes, I'll grind it finer; perhaps, God willing, they will learn to eat."

The next day Ramón arrived at the house very early in the morning to tell me that the chickens were very nervous and that some of them were going "Squawk, squawk," and turning around in circles. We went out and watched the chickens. They seemed perfectly normal, but some of them were very thin.

"I think it's your imagination," I told him. "In a few days they'll learn how to eat better."

"If God wishes," Ramón said, sadly.

That afternoon the first of the chickens died, and the next day two more died. We had a long conference at the chicken house; we doubled the Terramycin, changed the waterers, ground up new corn with new concentrate. I pointed out a crack in the roof to be fixed. "They have to sleep dry," I told him sternly. " I think they have cholera."

"Vaccinated chickens with cholera," Ramón said. "No, my poor babies are starving to death."

The next night, after all the farmers had left the house, Ramón came to talk; the fourth chicken had just died. "Before you came," he said, "well, you know how poor I was; I had nothing. But I was happy; I lived without worries. But now. My God, I am half crazy with worry." His voice broke and great tears swam in his eyes. "Oh, my poor chickens," he said. "Oh I don't want them to die."

I had talked to him before about how little by little he could increase his flock; I had told him that I hoped one day he would have one hundred chickens. Now, he said, this plan was terrifying. "I think it is God's will that I always live poorly, but now I think I will just raise the pair of pigs that you have promised to bring me and not have chickens."

"You can't let four lousy chickens wreck your life." I told him. "I don't think God is involved in this business; you have to consider this experience as a valuable lesson and keep trying."

"No one else has sick chickens," Ramón said. "Only this ignorant, brute *zambo* has sick chickens."

I had to go to Quito for seeds and chicken concentrate, and I talked to my boss, Eduardo Sotomayor, about the problem. Eduardo decided to take me back to Rio Verde and look things over. As we walked up the beach with Ramón to look at the chickens, I asked Eduardo to give a good inspirational talk in Spanish about "if at first you don't succeed," etc. Eduardo was magnificent, and Ramón listened intently, impaled on eloquence.

"Did I cut off too much beak?" I asked Eduardo at the chicken house.

"You could have cut off even more," Eduardo said.

"Tell Ramón in Spanish," I said. "He doesn't believe me; he thinks I ruined his chickens."

"But it's not the beaks that's wrong; the birds had cholera."

"Tell Ramón in Spanish," I said. "Tell him in your beautiful, clear Spanish so that he understands perfectly."

Eduardo took the last of the sick chickens back to Quito and sent me the results of the lab report—cholera. Passing Ramón's house a few days later, I stopped a minute to talk to Esther. Ramón's seven chickens were eating and dancing around. "Ramón just left," she told me. "He was cutting off the beaks of a couple of chickens that you missed before."

That night Ramón came by the house and apologized for the long doubts he had had about me. "I want to get started right away on the new chicken house," he said. "I'd like to buy forty-three of the new chickens to make an even fifty, and then after the corn is planted, build another chicken house. By June, God willing, I will have one hundred chickens. You know what I'm going to buy when I am rich?" he said, beginning to laugh with delight at the idea. "A pair of shoes. Oh my God. My God."

Quito, 1982

After twelve years of Ramón, four as a Peace Corps volunteer, eight as a business partner (a very different matter), we quarreled and I left the coastal jungles to live in Quito. What we quarreled about in this awful clash of cultures was rooted basically in the accident of color—black pride unable to feel endlessly dominated by white complacency, white middle-classness appalled finally to the point of anger by black stubbornness and Ramón's insistence on finding idiotically simple solutions to mildly complicated problems. We each made truth out of our prejudices and preconceptions. And there were other more serious things that fueled conflict. How, for instance, could I watch Ramón day after day spooning sugar over his avocado without feeling the first dim stirrings of madness?

This racial strangeness—Ramón's blackness, my whiteness, set up powerful forces that repelled and attracted, but the tensions became more unbearable with time; they were demoralizing but weak enough to have made the possibility of some final break unthinkable. We were condemned for life to a friendship that was half admiration, half irritation.

So we quarreled and because now I was old and tired and sick, I said to hell with it. I left the coast, left off farming, went to Quito to live but still under the power of those years in the jungle living with black people, I immediately wrote a book that tried to pierce the mystery of why my color and Ramón's color had made friendship between us so complicated, so explosive. In time we were reconciled but I stayed in Quito. If I were sure of anything it was that I would never go back to the squalor of the coast, never live again in a grass hut without running water or lights; and that never, never again would I allow myself to be dominated by someone like Ramón with his brutal and rural pragmatism. But if I often found him plain or stubborn or stupid, these were the traits, the neurotic scars of an early poverty, and so for all his abrasive ways he was never less than interesting to me who wished to see myself as a student of poverty.

By the end of the four years in which I lived on the edges of the gringo ghetto in Quito and during which we seldom met, we had been friends for over sixteen years. I had invested too much of my life in his to write him off. We weren't so much friends now as members of the same family. I had helped to raise his children or at any rate played the role of grandfather. In a weird reversal I realized that I needed Ramón more than he needed me. He was rich now; I still needed him to explain his country for me and to interpret a culture which each day I found less and less attractive. I had written three books about Ecuador by this time, feeling at the end of each that I understood everything less and that the universal poverty where I had chosen to live until I came to Quito was more and more confusing, more irrational, almost in many cases an affectation, freely chosen by a lumpen people to celebrate and publicly flaunt their anarchistic and self-destructive propensities.

Like many poor blacks who grew up isolated in the small villages or far beaches, Ramón, out of a need to feel his brain coming alive in the hellish tedium of jungle life, had learned to play with language; the sounds of words, the play of words, the scandalous meanings, the obscene ambiguities that made people howl with awe and admiration and led them to slap themselves. He was, admittedly, at a primitive, unschooled level, a kind of Nabokov. Almost everything that I really knew about South America at the gut level Ramón had explained to me. Not everything he said was clear. He wasn't cursed with the need to be consistent. One day he talked like Alexander Hamilton, the next, Che Guevara. I ended up as complicated as a Tinguely sculpture constructed out of bits and pieces from the continent's garbage dumps, all of it programmed to self-destruct at a near but uncertain moment. I lived in a reasonable context with all of Ramón's prejudices plus all my own.

One of Ramón's vices was his inability to guard his assets, to savor his treasures. He was spendthrift and like a gambler

211

ready to invest resources in unproven projects that suddenly and for no reason inflamed his enthusiasms. He would spend sums of money planting new experimental crops that bored him a month away from harvest. He bought farms or city lots that served no purpose in his life and gave him little pleasure. He jumped from scheme to scheme and because he was going through a period of good luck, he usually came out from his projects smelling of roses. I had come to Ecuador with a little money, my father had died at a crucial moment and left me a little more, and we had bought the land that then increased in value forty-fold and when finally sold had made Ramón rich. This was an awful fact that he could seldom accept, this truth that it was more than just his business genius and his willingness to work hard that had made him a millionaire in *sucres*. How irritating my presence must have been at those times when he wanted to see himself as a self-made man.

He now proceeded to gamble with his real treasures, and now his luck had begun to change.

Ramón sent his two children and their mother to Quito soon after I had gone there to live. More than anything in the world he wanted them to be highly educated. "Here is one of my dreams," he told me. "We are all sitting together at the dinner table and you and my son are talking English together, and I am sitting there nodding and smiling and not understanding a word but oh my God, how proud." It is one of Ramón's dreams that has come true. He enrolled them in one of the most expensive private schools in the country. One of the most expensive and one of the worst.

So now his family was divided and Ramón lived alone on the farm, sometimes for a few weeks at a time with a series of old women he had hired to wash his clothes and cook his meals. Every month he would drive seven hours across the country and up fifteen thousand feet through foggy Andean passes to visit his children and then, still not having slept, drive back to the coast, the only place he felt really at home.

There was another reason for Ramón's short visits that none of us in Quito knew at first; he had fallen in love with the nineteen year old daughter of one of the men who worked for him. He came up to talk to me about this complication one day. "You know that there hasn't been much of anything between Esther and me for years. And now I must leave her. I think in her heart she won't care though she'll probably scream and raise hell. Esther and I are finished, and if I leave her it's not to leave the children. I don't want to leave the children. I'll send them money every month, I'll come to see them, we'll take little trips together, eat out. They can come to Esmeraldas on their vacations. Martín, I'm getting old, and I'm lonesome in the house with no one to talk to. It's awful to be so alone; the nights after the sun sets are hell. And she's a good girl, Carmen, a simple country girl, absolutely honest in every way. And she cares for me as Esther never did."

"Listen Ramón, your family isn't like that patch of sesame you planted and then got bored with, that field of watermelons you didn't bother to harvest. The main thing is the children, " I said. "You can't control their feelings. They're too young to understand your taking up with another woman. They won't accept what they'll see as rejection and betrayal."

"Maybe not at first. They don't understand how life is yet, how people can change."

"Now you're messing with the emotions of people. How can those little kids handle Esther's tears?"

"Well, for one thing she could cry in private if she has to cry. But I know, I know; it's a serious move. I've been thinking and thinking about it."

"Does Esther know?"

"Not yet."

"And your mind is made up?"

"Yes we're living together."

"Well then, I think you should tell Esther immediately. She deserves better than hearing about the other woman from someone else."

"Yes." Ramón said, " I planned on telling her today, but I wanted to talk to you first."

"Why talk to me if your mind's made up? Well, the saying is: you do what you want and then you pay the price."

"What does that mean?"

"That there will be a price, that maybe you are trading your children for a few moments of red hot kisses."

"It's not like that," Ramón cried, "and I wouldn't do it if I weren't sure the children would understand in time."

"Wait until Esther gets through brainwashing them. You'll be the biggest monster since the dinosaurs. Women don't like being dumped, not even in this country where women are just so much shit."

"I'll give her some more money," Ramón said. "She's always liked money more than me."

"Don't talk like a complete ass-hole," I said. "Was it your money she was after when you were earning thirty cents a day?"

Ramón left and came back in a couple of hours. He was pale and shaken. "Holy God," he said, "what an extravaganza. She went out of her mind. Screaming, hysterics, gallons of tears. She was always a crier, but never like this, this flood of tears."

"In front of the children?"

"No, no," Ramón said. "They were in school. But you were right, she's going to work on them. I imagine for a while they're going to be cross with me. They're only going to hear her side of it."

A couple of years passed. The children who had been numbed by what they saw as the cold-blooded betrayal of everything that had given meaning to their lives, gradually developed an attitude toward their father. It was one of deep and unforgiving anger. Their foundation had been overturned and they felt alone and deserted, two fatherless black kids in a strange new city of prejudice. They started to call me father, and little Ramón, seven years old, told me a secret: he had used to kiss his father on the mouth and would I please from now on do the same. How soft the lips of a child. What had I ever done in life to deserve so beautiful a son?

On the coast Ramón had sold our farm and with his share of the money had bought another larger one, and came to live in Tachina where the river and the sea met and where he operated a fleet of motorized canoes, buying and selling shrimp. He built a cement house on the beach and bought a color television set. He bought a new pick-up truck, a pure bred bull for his farm up the coast, a fancy little portable light plant for a farm he never slept in. He spent thousands on a new corral built of hardwood and cement. He was making lots of money. And what joy. He was doing it on his own.

Ramón was busy for a couple of months and didn't appear in Quito, but one morning, having left at three a.m., he drove up from the coast and came to my apartment. Esther owned a restaurant now, it was just around the corner. Ever since the day of the big cry and the wild screaming Ramón had been reluctant to face her. He asked me to get his children and bring them to him. I went down into the street and by chance met Ramón's daughter, Martha, who was on her way to baby-sit for one of the teachers from her school. "Hey, Martita, your father's here, waiting to see you up in my apartment."

"I'm busy," she said. "I haven't got time." She got a cold dead sullen look on her face.

"You can't go up for five minutes? Come on now, Martha."

"I'm already late," she said. "I've got to go."

"Martha don't be wicked."

"Does he think he can come up here a couple of times a year and find us just waiting to run into him?"

"He's working hard down there to send you money every month. Sometimes he can't get away."

Martha shrugged and walked away from me. Over her shoulder she called back, "Tell him I'm busy."

Young Ramón was asleep in the upstairs part of the restaurant where the family lived now, trying to save money. Ten o'clock of a Saturday morning; he still had two hours of sleep coming. I went up and shook him awake, or half awake. "Get up, get up you lazy kid. Your father's here to see you." I shook and pummeled, and pulled at the blankets, and after a time he sat up in bed and I left him to dress.

Back in the apartment Ramón waited. A half hour passed and feeling that something awful was now happening, I began to make excuses for the children. "Martita's baby-sitting. I don't think she can leave right now. Probably later. And

Ramoncito, well, you know how he loves to sleep. I think I'll go down and wake him up again."

Back at the restaurant things were progressing. Ramoncito was now sitting on the edge of the bed in his underwear holding a shoe in one hand. He was still incapable of speech, still more asleep than awake. "Come on, Ramón, move a little faster. Your father's waiting." He sat there staring at his shoe as though he weren't quite sure what it was.

When I went back Ramón was pacing up and down in the street outside the apartment. He was extremely nervous, almost distraught and kept passing both hands over his face as though trying to erase some inner pain. "He's coming," I said. "Not very fast but he's coming. A sort of miracle really, he's dressing in his sleep."

Ramón said nothing and we waited.

We waited another fifteen minutes. "I'd better go shake him up again," I said.

"No," Ramón said, "never mind." He walked over to his pick-up, leaned his head up against it, put both hands on the top of the cab and wailed in a voice that held both disbelief and realization, "My God, I've lost my children." When he looked at me a minute later the tears were gushing from his eyes and his voice was choked with sobs. "It's not their fault," I think he said. "They're not to blame."

At this moment young Ramón appeared walking slowly up the street tucking his shirt tails into his pants. Ramón saw him, walked across the street, knelt before him and held him close. He was still sobbing; he said something to his son, then got up abruptly and walked back to the pick-up. We shook hands. "I'm going back now, and I guess I won't be coming up much anymore. Just as well. A couple more days like this would finish me off. I don't blame them, but how could she? That bitch, how could she rob her children of their father?" He shook his head like a man who has just been slugged. He waved at young Ramón who had just begun to cross the street to us, gave me a bleak half-smile and drove away.

After Ramón left us to drive back to the coast, I walked around the corner with his son to Esther's restaurant. She was splitting into halves the heads of sea perch and making fish soup for the luncheon trade. "Has he gone so soon?" she asked me, tense and angry. I nodded without speaking. Ramón's grief lived in my mind, and I was too choked up to speak. I pushed Ramoncito in behind the counter, said, "Eat," and went outside to stand in the sun and think. Ramón, the tough jungle fighter whose motto for years had been, "Nobody fucks with Ramón Prado." How unbearable to see someone who is truly tough when he cracks up.

There were very few customers in the restaurant—two mechanics drinking beer, the old fellow, a carpenter, who came in every morning for his bowl of *chupe*. Esther cooked up something for her son and came outside to stand with me in the sunshine. "Ramón says his father was crying when he drove off."

"Have you ever seen Ramón cry?" I asked, choking. I turned my face away from her.

"No, never," she said. "Not in fifteen years."

"And me? Have you ever seen me cry?"

"Well, no, I don't think so."

"Then look," I said, turning my face and showing the tears streaming down it. "It was terrible to see, Esther."

"Don't talk to me about it." Esther said. "I don't want to hear."

"Well, he won't be coming up any more," I said. "Does that make you feel better?"

"Let him suit himself. If he comes, if he doesn't come, what difference does it make to me?" And now Esther who was a crier had begun to cry.

"I'm thinking of the children. I'm thinking why is it Ramón who always has to come up **here**? Think about it: fourteen hours of driving, without sleep. Why can't the children go down there?"

"That's why, because they're children. Ramón is only nine. I won't have them wandering lost on the streets of Esmeraldas like orphans."

"Then let them fly. Ramón lives five minutes from the airport. The first time he can meet them when they get off the

217

plane. After that when they go down they'll know where he lives, they can walk to his house."

"And the money?"

"I'll buy the tickets this time. After that it's between you and Ramón. OK?"

"Esther stood there thinking. She wiped her face and gave a little burst of laughter. "Tell me, Martin, why do you cry for Ramón's tears? You never cry for mine."

"Oh, but Esther, you're an Ecuadorian woman. You're so much garbage in the social system. That's your job, to cry. How can I cry for you when you're just doing your job?"

"Wait," she said. "I'm learning how not to cry." She inhaled, then nodded. "All right, they'll have to go down Friday afternoon after school. And how will he know they're coming?"

The next day the plane took me to Tachina—seven hours on the road, thirty minutes by air. It was that trip that I had thought never to make again. But I made it to tell Ramón to meet his children at the airport.

I stepped out into a tropical ambience that, until I took a first rich breath of coastal air, I had only half known how much I mourned having lost. From the plane's door, out past a wall of pasture grass and scattered trees, ebony, amarillo, guayacan, past a few tall coco palms that grew at the river's edge, the town of Esmeraldas across the river, white and spreading, throbbed in the brutal light, its squalor hidden by distance. It looked in the squareness and whiteness of its buildings and the vivid green of the pastures in the hills above the town like a child's invention made of blocks and match-boxes. To the right across the whole horizon the Pacific spread, mud colored near the shore, farther out clear tropic greens and blues. Behind us lay the gently curving hills cleared on their lower slopes of trees and planted to pasture, the white spots of brahma cattle sharp against the green. The hills had the curves of sleeping women.

Nothing had changed; everything was just the way it used to be—warm, soft, languorous, sensual. It grabbed my heart and lifted it up, and I stood in the door of the plane, ten seconds into my coastal journey thinking, "But what the hell am I doing living in Quito when here is where I belong?" and the conviction was instantly born that I must come back immediately and live here by the river until I died.

Ramón lived near the ocean-river beach on the other side of the airport, but I didn't know just where. I walked around the end of the airfield to the old dirt road that runs up the coast and where years before as a Peace Corps volunteer I had walked in and out from the fishing village where I lived. It was April or May and the grass was tall and just barely beginning to turn yellow; it leaned out over the road spilling seeds. Everything caught in the thick luminous light of the tropics glowed in a kind of super-color, new, improved, Ektachrome. Puddles in the road, emerald green at the edges with algae, caught and held a brazen sun like a scattered line of stars thrown down ahead of me. I began to sweat.

A black man in his sixties walked toward me on the road—torn pants and shirt, barefoot. Two or three long branches, firewood, lay balanced across one shoulder. "*Buenos días.* Can you tell me where Ramón Prado lives?"

"*Claro,* just keep walking down this road, about a mile. It's a yellow house with a TV antenna and with a tall fence around it. But Don Martín, don't you remember me?"

It had been fifteen years since I had walked down this road on the edge of Tachina, but didn't I almost remember him? I took a wild guess, "But *claro,* you used to take me across the river in your canoe when I was trying to get to Rio Verde." He grinned at being remembered and grinning lost that little itch of familiarity; he had lost all his teeth.

"Yes, and don't you remember, you gave me some of those fine gringo chickens." Ah yes, I thought and you were one of those who never paid. But I forgave him now. It made me feel good to be remembered, made me feel famous.

We talked for a few minutes about how it had been then, and he said that all in all it hadn't changed much, at least not for the better. The town was still poor, poorer even now because the river had carried half of it away, all the river gardens on the bottom land, the groves of coconuts, most of the mangos. "And where do you live now?" he asked me.

"Well the truth is, I'd like to come back here and live. Aren't there some little farms around here for sale?"

"Why yes," he said, pointing just across the fence to the land that later I would buy. "This, right here, Valencia's pastures. He's old now, a disgraceful old shit, but I think he'll finally sell. They robbed him of all his cows a few months back. He's mad and disgusted."

"Ah," I said, "so Tachina is still a town of thieves."

The old man nodded. "He stood in the window one midnight with a full moon, old Valencia, and watched them steal his cows, stood there with a loaded gun afraid to shoot because one of the thieves was his own son."

I moved around past the man and started off again. "Listen, Don Martín, we're in a more dangerous time now, old veterans like you shouldn't be walking alone like this. The young scum from Esmeraldas paddle over here in their stolen bongos and do just about anything they want. Not two weeks ago here on the road just after dark a man was beat up and robbed, and back there at the edge of town one of the fishermen's wives was dragged into the bushes and raped."

I walked on up the road toward Ramón's yellow house feeling more excited that I'd felt for months, thinking, "Oh man, this place is **wicked**!" And the two reasons now why I wanted to come back, the child's reason, the river on my left, swift and tropical that was a symbol of free flowing freedom and innocence, and the old man's reason, the mystery, the appeal, the excitement of living close again to man's capacity for evil, both lived side by side giving color and drama to the other. There is a kind of softness in the tropics, a slack disorganized beauty that loosens the brain, that dissolves moral tendencies not tightly held. For me, without this new other thing, this hint of menace, living here could turn out to be as tiresome as living within the pinks and golds of a ten-cent postcard. And so now to be reminded that I would be returning to a place where I would live in the shadow of violence, hit me with a little shock of joy; it brought me to life.

If on one level my pleasure in anticipating the possibility of danger was a little like the thrill of a race car driver who feels more alive when he offers his life to fate, this was probably the least important of the reasons for coming back. I was an old man rushing toward my sixty-eighth birthday, and I had not aged gracefully. My feelings about life were sour, cynical, filled with despair. I no longer believed that man was essentially good or that he was capable of creating a decent world. What man could create with exquisite efficiency was **hell**; man with his Hitlers, his Stalins, his atom bombs. For twenty years, feeling at first that poverty was simply a manifestation of our inability to forge a humane economic system, I had tried to write about poor people as victims of others' greed. To a degree this is still true I think, but each year I understood less and less about why a quarter of the people in the world so often sleep with empty stomachs.

It now occurred to me that it was man's evil that interested me much more than his poverty. After you had lived with poor people for so many years it finally became as hopeless, as inscrutable, as boring as having to listen to the screams month after month of your neighbor as he very slowly died of cancer.

Poverty was a thing, a permanent condition; evil was like chancres, the symptoms of a social disease.

Living in the high altitude of Quito where I found it more and more difficult to breathe, moving among expatriates in the complacent and goofy foreign colony I felt half dead, like an old Ford truck with a hundred and fifty thousand miles behind it rattling down identical streets on a foolish and useless route. We don't know how we are going to die, but at the end of my route I thought I could make out a wheel chair, a trained nurse, and that bottle labelled Overdose.

Going back to the coast would open up my life to the possibility, at least of a surprise ending. Man's badness, that badness that might touch me, that might, but probably wouldn't, had now become fascinating. I wanted to go back where I could observe evil in its primitive state and be close to the poverty that spawned it. That extreme poverty that strips a man of even the clothes to cover his body also strips him of his social pretenses, his hypocrisies, his disguises, his graces. Reduced to nothing but needs, wants, hungers, powerless, faced each day with the possibility that he will go hungry or that his children will sicken with diseases he will be unable to cure, half sick always from malnutrition, intestinal parasites, or chronic malaria, he must find solutions to the problem of existing in ways that do not necessarily exclude thievery or violence. And because in all probability he has lost a part of his intelligence during those early years of childhood malnutrition, his solutions are sometimes as pure, direct, unsubtle, and painful as the slash of a machete.

A light breeze from the ocean moved over the grass, and a long line of pelicans appeared off on the left flying just above the trees on the shore line. I walked up the road another kilometer and found Ramón's house and Ramón inside eating lunch. He lived in the yellowest house I had seen since leaving Brazil. Yellow inside, yellow out. That terrible woman who had stolen him away turned out to be as Ramón had said she was, a sweet, simple, very serious country girl, and what he hadn't thought to tell me, beautiful.

I gave them the news that the children were coming down. Ramón was delighted, Carmen frightened of this meeting in which she might be cast as the temptress, the destroyer of happy homes.

Finally I told him I was sick of Quito and asked him what he thought about my buying the Valencia pasture and coming back to live on the coast. "I'd like the idea very much," Ramón said. "I never thought you were very happy up there. And I know the place is for sale. The old man stopped by here a month ago and begged me to buy it."

In twenty minutes it was all settled, even the details. I would remain in Quito, hidden, while Ramón bought the land. If Valencia smelled a gringo, the price would double. We would put title to the farm in Ramoncito's name to screw the government out of death taxes. There was no sense in repairing the old house by the road, better to build a new one. With iron grates at the windows. "Get used to the idea," Ramón said. "When you move down here they are going to rob you of everything."

Moritz Thomsen

Moritz Thomsen was born in Los Angeles in 1915 and studied at the University of Washington, the University of Oregon and Columbia University. He served as a bombadier in the Eighth Air Force of the United States Army during World War II. After 20 years as a farmer in California he joined the Peace Corps. Thomsen served as an agricultural expert in rural coastal Ecuador. He wrote articles about his experiences which were regularly printed in the San Francisco Chronicle and became the basis of his first book.

Thomsen is the author of three books about his life in South America:

> *Living Poor, A Peace Corps Chronicle*
>> (University of Washington Press 1969)
> *The Farm on the River of Emeralds*
>> (Houghton Mifflin 1978)
> *The Saddest Pleasure, A Journey on Two Rivers*
>> (Graywolf Press 1990)

Thomsen received the Washington State Governor's Award and in 1990 he became the first recipient of the Paul Cowan Award, the National Council of Returned Peace Corps Volunteers prize for non-fiction. He lives in Guayaquil, Ecuador, and has completed a fourth book now simply known as *MS #4*. His story, "Ramón" is excerpted from *Living Poor* and his latest unpublished manuscript.

Editor's note:
Moritz Thomsen died in Guayaquil in August 1991.

Praise !

"Geraldine Kennedy's choices cannot be faulted. I don't know of any other volume that has captured the Peace Corps spirit as insightfully . . ."
The Washington Post

"The writers share the belief that people of different cultures can come together in mutual appreciation and respect for their differences, though the experiences they describe are at times wrenching. A superb collection . . ."
The Atlanta Journal Constitution

" 'Pretty exotic' will be many a reader's conclusion, but so will 'thoroughly human,' i.e., funny, raffish, tragic, cruel, . . . this is a powerful, engrossing collection." ***Booklist, The American Library Association***

"The collection contains a surprising amount of humor for a book grounded in cultural turmoil, global poverty, linguistic confusion, and a decent amount of tragedy. . . . a crash course in cultural relativism while capturing the peculiar sights, struggles, and smells of distant places." ***Village View***

"These are real writers at work, who have observed so keenly the arcana of the cultures they lived in, and written it all down, that you can begin to feel overwhelmed . . ."
RPCV Writers

". . . a collection of first-rate fiction . . . a veritable treasure trove of excellent prose . . . refreshing and uplifting . . ."
RAPPORT, The West Coast Review of Books

". . . full of unexpected insights . . . literate . . . highly readable stories"
Kliatt Young Adult Paperback Book Guide

". . . required reading for everyone considering cross-cultural service."
WMSC Voice
Women's Missionary and Service Commission of the Mennonite Church

"These Peace Corps tales succeed in illuminating a potpourri of cultures, with little self-pity, an understandable amount of frustration and a leavening of humor."
Small Press, The Magazine of Independent Publishing